BEHIND THE MYSTERY

BEHIND THE MYSTERY

Top Mystery Writers

INTERVIEWED BY

STUART KAMINSKY

PHOTOGRAPHED BY

LAURIE ROBERTS

HotHouse
PRESS

Library of Congress Cataloging-in-Publication Data

Kaminsky, Stuart M.
  Behind the mystery: top mystery writers interviewed / written by Stuart Kaminsky and photographed by Laurie Roberts.
     p. cm.
   ISBN 0-9755245-2-6
  1. Detective and mystery stories, American—History and criticism—Theory, etc. 2. Novelists, American—20th century—Interviews. 3. Detective and mystery stories—Authorship. I. Title.
   PS374.D4K36 2005
   813'.08720905—dc22
                                2005015289

Printed in the United States of America

Book design by Mark Soliday

Hot House Press
760 Cushing Highway
Cohasset, MA 02025
www.hothousepress.com

Thanks

Needless to say, this experience has been an amazing ride. Over the last four years, I've spent weeks traveling around the country meeting and talking with profoundly intelligent and private people. My thanks go out to all these writers who welcomed me into their homes with such sincerity and warmth and allowed me to photograph their private lives. It was an experience I will not soon forget.

As you can see from Lawrence Block's apartment view, this project began in 2001 before the World Trade Center fell. I was scheduled for an eighteen-day trip to shoot nine writers in eight states throughout the West and Mid-West. A few days into my itinerary, I found myself watching footage of memorials and news broadcasts with Ann Rule and Joseph Wambaugh. The collective response to the attacks, including my own, was startling. I realized there comes a time to put down the camera.

There are a few people who have made this project possible whom I'd like to thank. Most importantly, I'd like to thank my parents, Alan and Laura Roberts, for always supporting me and for believing in my vision. You've consistently helped make my dreams a reality. I'd also like to thank Jon Porter for your relentless belief in my photography and in me, not to mention all the times I've asked for your help as an assistant, printer and retoucher. You light my way. My thanks go out to Stuart Kaminsky for knowing which doors to knock on and when to keep knocking! I'd also like to thank Amy Boyle for her significant help in finishing this wonderful book and Mark Soliday for his excellent designing abilities and for his patience during my maiden voyage. Thank you, Natalie Obermaier, Jeremy Chrzan, Nicholas Katona, Enid Perll, Wes Roberts, Randy Riggs, Abbi Russal, Wayne and Susan Barcomb, Seth Sherman, and all the rest of you who have supported me throughout the last four years and always. And especially thanks to David Replogle, my publisher, for giving me a chance to prove myself to everyone, including myself.

Laurie Roberts

Dedication

To the memory of my friend, mentor, my inspiration, Evan Hunter.
—Stuart M. Kaminsky

Table of Contents

Introduction

In my almost thirty years as a writer, primarily of mysteries, I have met and become friends—often very close friends—with dozens of writers.

When writers get together we seldom talk about many of the things in which we are most interested: our parents and heritage, lifestyles, thoughts about religion and politics, what we think about, what we have done and what we still wish to accomplish. We eat, drink, trade jokes, exchange gossip and wish each other well on our next book.

I have often wanted to sit down with my friends and just get to know them better; get to know them in their own environment; get to know what they think and feel about things we never discuss and hopefully ask some questions they're not usually asked.

So that is what I did for this book.

I teamed up with another friend, photographer Laurie Roberts. We decided to go ahead with the book even before we had a publisher. We visited the writers separately, and while I tell my story in description and conversation, Laurie adds hers intimate portraits of the writers in their homes.

Whenever possible, I traveled to the writer's home (which meant a lot of traveling). I talked to Ann Rule and Michael Connelly in my home. I traveled the Bayou country of Louisiana to interview James Lee Burke, along the Rio Grande River to talk to Tony Hillerman in New Mexico, the coast of South Carolina to sit with Mickey Spillane, to Louisville for Sue Grafton, Beverly Hills with Faye and Jonathan Kellerman, and a mountaintop in California to talk to Martin Cruz Smith.

So, how were these specific authors chosen? There was no plan, no agonizing about any kind of balance of genre, gender, region, age or anything else. I picked my friends. Fortunately, I know some remarkably interesting and creative people. I thought fans of these writer-friends might want to know something about them as people, not just as famous writers. I thought I could add a dimension to the book because I am one of them—a writer and a lover of mysteries.

There are many writers left out of this book whom I would like to have included. But there was just not enough room and time. Making the final decision was difficult; however, I was determined to stay with writers I considered friends. These are people I have always found fascinating, and I could be certain that their personal stories, like their fictional ones, would draw us in with their wit, insight and honesty.

I have read the work of all the people in this book, and I am a fan. I'll continue to be a fan and, I hope, a friend.

Stuart M. Kaminsky

SUE GRAFTON

The hard thing about death is that nothing ever changes. The hard thing about life is that nothing stays the same.
—*J Is For Judgment* by Sue Grafton

Sue, looking comfortably disheveled, meets me at the door of her expansive, stately mansion in Louisville. I've known Sue Grafton and her husband for more than twenty years, before the birth and success of her lead character, Kinsey Milhorne. I remember one time several decades ago when I invited Sue to a conference I was hosting in Chicago and she had to decline because she simply couldn't afford it.

Things change.

"They're fixing the pond," she says. "Want to take a look?"

We walk to the end of the huge three-story house, in which Steve and Sue live alone with frequent visits from their children. When we make the turn we can see four workmen at a large stone pond with a little waterfall.

Sue and Steve have been married for twenty-two years. He holds a Ph.D. in Philosophy and Physics and teaches part-time at the University of Louisville and at the University of California-Santa Barbara. An avid weightlifter, he has a passion for Quantum Mechanics, golf, cooking and was a writing partner with Sue when they worked in television in the 1970's and 80's.

Before meeting Steve, she had a set of rocky relationships with men. She married at eighteen, had a daughter, Leslie, and while pregnant, left her husband. Her first husband raised Leslie whom Sue didn't see again till her daughter was seventeen. Sue did raise her son Jay. She met Al Schmidt on a blind date when she was twenty-two and married him soon after. After selling her second novel to Hollywood, Sue took her children and left. Her now ex-husband sued for custody and lost. He had not wanted the divorce.

But that is twenty-five years in the past.

Inside the massive house, the wooden floors echo with our footsteps as I follow her. It is raining slightly now, but the windows are large and the house bright.

In Sue's second-floor office which is light wood, modern and uncluttered, holds a no-nonsense metal desk dominated by a computer and very little on the walls and bookshelves.

We sit. Sue glances at the words on her computer screen.

"I'm just getting into tracking my family back. I'm on the hunt for my mother's mother. Both of my grandfathers were Presbyterian missionaries in China and my grandfather Harnsberger married a woman whose name, I believe, was Lanie Gillespie. My mother, Vivian, was the only child of that union. She was born in West Virginia in 1908 and raised in China. She always claimed I was born in Spruce, West Virginia."

"What do you know about your grandparents?"

"The story is my grandfather was out on horseback preaching in the provinces of China when my grandmother Harnsberger had an ectopic pregnancy with twins and died. When he got back from his trek, he married a woman named Agnes Lacy Wood. My grandfather Grafton lost his wife, too. He married Mary Woods, Agnes's cousin."

"You've explored Kinsey's family history in *J Is For Judgment*."

Sue is at her desk. I'm in a chair next to it. She looks over her shoulder at some old books on a shelf. The dust jackets are worn.

They are the mysteries written by her father, C.W. Grafton. He practiced law in Louisville for forty years specializing in municipal bonds and finding time to write four mystery novels, *The Rat Began to Gnaw the Rope*, *The Rope Began to Hang the Butcher*, *Beyond a Reasonable Doubt* and *My Name is Christopher Nagel*. He died in 1982.

"Yes," Sue says. "Kinsey discovers part of her own family history because I think we, our sense of self, is formed by the stories we hear about our birth and the lives of our parents and grandparents. New or different information will shift your whole perception not only of yourself but of all your ancestors."

"Kinsey is, among other things, funny."

"Humor comes out in writing," Sue says as she and Steve clear the table. "Humor is about telling the truth and most of us are too polite to do that. I can't do it to order. What gets me to humor is getting so lost in character you let them take over."

"Are you a practicing Presbyterian?"

"No, but I don't disbelieve. I do pray for my children. I'd like to feel that there is something that takes care of them when I'm not present."

"In your writing you use the words 'shadow' and 'ego' fairly often. What do you mean?"

"When I was doing *J Is For Judgment*, I did phone therapy for three months with an analyst, Jungian stuff that had seemed abstract and mysterious before but started to make sense. Starting with *J Is For Judgment*, I let my dark side, my shadow, take over. I gave up control and didn't worry about writing well. I didn't care about pleasing people. I didn't care about turning the manuscript in on time. I just let go of what I call ego issues. Ego is the part of each of us that wants to be patted on the back, praised, the part of us that keeps saying, 'Me, me, me. Like me. Love me.' When ego is in charge, you want to please others, not yourself. If you let your dark side or your shadow take over, it doesn't care what others think or want. It just lets everything you hold back come out and the hell with the consequences."

"You have one sister."

"Ann. She's three years older, a retired librarian in Cincinnati."

"Not far from here."

"Right. In fact, we share a cat. We have a time-share cat. When we come to Kentucky, we either drive to Cincinnati or she drives down with her husband David and the cat, Bridget. I can't resist cats."

The phone rings. Sue excuses herself and begins talking, giving advice, asking about children, listening, comfortable.

When she hangs up, she says, "That was my daughter Leslie in Virginia Beach. Leslie is

forty-two. She's head of medical records at a psychiatric hospital. She has two daughters, Erin, who is seventeen, and Kinsey is nine. We spent last Thanksgiving at their house. I've also got a son, Jay, who's forty-one and my youngest, my daughter Jamie, is thirty-six. Jay's not married. He lives in Ventura and does construction, carpentry, wallpapering. He builds movie and television sets. Robert lives in Vallejo, near San Francisco."

"When did you first feel you were really a writer?"

"It took me five books before I started to feel I was getting it right. It takes years to get there. I started as a 'mainstream' novelist. My first published book was *Keziah Dane*. It was actually the fourth book I'd written. In 1967, *The Lolly-Madonna War*, the fifth book I had written, was published."

"Do you read a lot?"

"I always have three books on an airplane. Suppose you finish one, start another and hate it. You need that third."

"You went to college here in Louisville."

"I went to the University of Louisville for a year and then transferred to Western Kentucky State Teachers College. I didn't get a lot out of college and it amuses me that these institutions want me to give them money, which I won't do."

Sue suggests we break for lunch. We go back downstairs to the big, modern kitchen where she makes sandwiches from leftover meatloaf and calls Steve in to join us. We talk while we eat.

"You worked in television before you started novel writing."

"Yeah, a lot. Movies for television."

"You won a Christopher Award in 1979 for your script *Walking through the Fire*."

"That was one. More Coke?"

Sue's television movie credits also include *Sex and the Single Parent, Mark, I Love You, Nurse*, and with husband Steve she adapted two Agatha Christie novels, *Caribbean Mystery* and *Sparkling Cyanide*.

"You've said you learned a lot about writing from working in film and television."

"The structure of a good novel is basically the same structure as a good movie," she says. "When I was writing movies for television, I could lay out any premise in seven acts flat. My mind began to work that way. When it came to writing mysteries, I knew how to organize the narrative. Hollywood also taught me how to write scenes. I see my novels as films as I write them."

"You write every day?"

"Yes, because it keeps me connected to the book. During the Thanksgiving and Christmas holidays I get away from daily writing, and it kills me. I just pray I'll remember what I was talking about or thinking when I sit down to write again."

"You've said you never want to see Kinsey on film."

"Never."

"Even if you wrote the script, produced, could cast and direct?"

"I don't want an actress' face attached to the part of Kinsey. I am Kinsey. Your wife is Kinsey. Your daughter is Kinsey. Kinsey is whoever you want her to be, not Sigourney Weaver."

Sue takes a drink from a can of Coke, looks out the window, pauses and says, "The minute Hollywood gives you a dollar, it's all over."

Steve goes back to the greenhouse. Sue and I move back up to her office.

"You had a difficult childhood."

"It was a perfect childhood for a writer," she says leaning back. "Raised by alcoholic parents. I drink a little wine, but I'm careful with it. You can't write hung over. Well, I can't."

"So who took care of you when you were growing up?"

"I did. My father practiced law most days of his life with a fifth of whiskey under his belt. My mother was 4'11" and never weighed more than ninety-eight pounds. My mother committed suicide. She had cancer of the throat. It was a long, ugly story. She wasn't going to put up with it. She died on my twentieth birthday. I'm still trying to understand what that means."

"Your birthday . . ."

"And her death day. Symbolism. Perfect for a writer."

"Do you write fast?"

"I shoot for two pages a day. Sometimes I do three or five. I wish I were more productive, more prolific. I just tap away at it day after day. I'm not fast."

"You are actually approaching the end of the Alphabet. Are you thinking ahead to Z?"

"I never think ahead. My strength is that I stay focused, and I don't worry about anything that isn't right there in front of me. The joy of the alphabet is that the challenge is so enormous. I liken it to a marathon, twenty-six miles, and I know I'm always pushing through to something I didn't think I could do."

We are finished. It is beginning to get dark and the rain has started. I want to get back to my hotel room and go over my notes and tapes. Before I leave, I turn off the recorder and say, "You're language can be very colorful. I'll cut out some of the more colorful words."

Sue gets up, smiles, holds out her hand and says, "I don't give a _ _ _ _."

ELMORE LEONARD

"I'm Chilli Palmer. I'm Ernesto Palmair. I was Chilli the Shylock, Chilli the Shark and I'm Chilli the Notorious K.M.A."

Sin Russell said, "Shit." He said, "You notorious, huh? What's K.M.A.?"

"Kiss My Ass," Chilli said in the man's face, "a name I was given on the street. How can I help you?"

Sin didn't answer, by his look trying to decide if he'd been disrespected.
—*Be Cool* by Elmore Leonard

Elmore Leonard, known as 'Dutch' to his friends, is lean and casually dressed. His trademark well-trimmed gray beard and welcoming smile greet me on a crisp Fall afternoon.

"This is the kind of weather I like," he says as he leads me through the door of his suburban Detroit home into a bright, sunny entryway. To the right, a large living room is flooded with light from large windows through which you can see an expansive, well-groomed lawn.

The furniture is French in style, elegant, tasteful, everything perfectly neat.

The only oddity is a large wooden desk in the middle of the room that doesn't match the other furniture. A large typewriter sits in the middle of stacks of paper.

He offers me a cup of coffee and explains that his wife Christine is away for the day. His first wife, Joan, with whom he had five children, died in 1993.

"You work in your living room?" I ask.

He sits behind his desk in a brown leather chair with dark wooden arms and looks out the window.

"Lots of room, good view. I've got an office in another room but I feel comfortable here."

"You don't have a computer," I say sitting at a chair across the desk.

"I type my manuscripts on this typewriter," he says nodding at the desk, "but I actually work on these." He points to a yellow legal-sized lined pad. "I have been writing in longhand ever since I sold my first story fifty years ago. I can write a line and cross it out, and then keep going once I feel the rhythm of it kick in and then go as far as I can. I wrote in longhand not to preserve a lost art, but in order to close out quicker, as I am writing and rewriting. I recently wrote something for *Esquire* on the lost art of writing by hand, the lost art of the oratory of cobalt. The article ran not in type but in my handwriting."

I say, "For me the problem with writing by hand, which I used to do, was I wound up doing too much cutting and pasting. I had this weird looking pile with Scotch tape all over it and paragraphs moved around."

"But when you compose on your computer and delete, it's gone, unless you print it out."

"Or save it," I say.

"Yeah. But then you're probably saving too much, more than you need. It's that mechanical process that turns me off. That's what it is." Leonard adds, "I rewrite as I go along so that as those yellow pages start to pile up, I'm always going back for one reason or another and

rewriting a page. People will say, 'But then you have to retype that whole page.' I say, 'Yes, but every time I do, something good seems to happen, so I don't mind retyping the page.' Or they'll say, 'You can write faster on a word processor.' I say, 'Why do I want to write faster?' Speed has nothing to do with it. Speed doesn't give you the ideas to put down."

"Do you have days that you consider really great days?"

"If I get five pages, that's a good day. When I get into the book, two-thirds into the book, I'll do more than five pages cause now we're moving. Most often when I have a problem it's in backstory, because I don't want to tell the backstory. I want somebody else to think about it or tell it to somebody else. I like to intercut the scenes and keep it moving."

Elmore Leonard's nickname, "Dutch" is because he is a life-long baseball fan, and back in the 50's there was a knuckle ball pitching major leaguer named Emil "Dutch" Leonard. His friends, who thought 'Elmore' was not the name of a real man, dubbed him 'Dutch,' and it stuck.

He stretches languidly and looks out at the lawn. A flock of small black birds momentarily pepper the sky.

"When did you know you were going to be a writer?"

Dutch smiles and shakes his head. "When I was in fifth grade. I wrote a World War I play inspired by *All Quiet on the Western Front*. We put it on in a classroom using the rows of desks

as a no-man's-land. I remember a coward, and a girl and references to barbed wire. After that I stopped writing and read, read, read. When I got to college, I wrote a couple of short stories with no particular direction. I got rejected and decided I'd have to pick a market and go about writing as a profession. It was either crime or Westerns and in the 50's Westerns were big even before television. I picked Westerns because I thought the stories would have a better chance of being picked up for the movies. To put it simply, I've been motivated from the beginning by the opportunity to make money."

"What did you know about Westerns when you started writing them?"

"Nothing," he says with a smile. "I researched, read books about Arizona and New Mexico in the 1880's. I learned about Apaches, the cavalry, cowboys, guns, even what kind of coffee they drank. I used it all, even subscribed to *Arizona Highways* for locations. If I needed a canyon, I'd thumb through the pages and find one and read the caption to learn what was growing up the side, what trees were there. By the end of the 50's the market for Westerns disappeared because of television."

"So, how did you make a living?"

"For seven years I worked for an advertising agency, wrote Chevrolet ads to supplement my fiction writing income. I had sold thirty short stories and five novels. The first short story I wrote was "Trail of the Apache." It was published in *Argosy Magazine* in December 1951. A few of the novels, *3:10 To Yuma* and *The Tall T* were made into pretty good movies. Then I wrote *Hombre*. It took me two years to write it and I got paid $1,250. To keep the money coming in while I wrote more novels and stories, I freelanced writing industrial and educational movies for Britannica. I wrote movies about the settling of the Mississippi River Valley, Spain, whatever

they wanted. Then I wrote a crime novel, *The Big Bounce* and sent it to the Swanson Agency. I got a call telling me I was going to be rich. My agent got eighty-four rejections on both coasts, but eventually, after I strengthened the plot, it sold as a movie and then as a paperback to Gold Medal Books."

"The movie was a success?"

"The movie," he says leaning forward, his coffee cup in hand, "was awful."

"Have you ever been really satisfied with a movie made from one of your books?"

"*Get Shorty*," he says. "It was released as a comedy. I told the director, Barry Sonnenfeld, that I didn't write comedy and he said it was a funny book. I remember telling Sonnenfeld two years before the production of *Get Shorty* that I hope he doesn't cut to another character to get a reaction after someone delivers a line. I told him to let the audience react. And he remembered that."

"Wait a minute. *Maximum Bob* is one of the funniest novels I've read."

"Yeah," Dutch says holding up a hand, "but the characters aren't trying to be funny."

Dutch agrees to some quick questions.

Kaminsky: What about the other adaptations of your novels?
Leonard: I've been satisfied with most of them, *Out of Sight* for example and *Jackie Brown*.

You've got a big backlist. Is everything in print?
Dell just bought my entire backlist for 1.65 million dollars. They're going to bring them out five at a time. They're going to do the Westerns first.

What do you see as the most important part of your novels and screenplays?
Character. It's nice to have a good plot, but the plot, for me, follows the character.

Anyone in your family a writer?
My mother wrote three short stories.

Your father?
He was with General Motors, head of the Chevrolet market analysis department, a mid-level job. I was born in New Orleans on October 11, 1925. We moved to Dallas and then Oklahoma City and wound up in Detroit when I was ten. My dad eventually quit GM to take on a dealership in New Mexico. Six months later he had a heart attack and died. He was fifty-six.

College?
Right here in Detroit, the University of Detroit. I graduated when I was twenty-three. I had joined the Seabees during World War II right after I got out of high school. I was stationed in the Admiralty Islands near New Guinea. After college, I got a job and got married. I was at that age. Everybody was getting married, and picking out their dishes. That was the thing to do.

What do your boys do?
Two of them are in advertising. One has his own agency. They do a lot of work for Volkswagen and Audi.

Do any of your sons write fiction?
One of my sons is writing a book. He wrote a half dozen screenplays and got nowhere with them.

You have some favorite writers?
Hemingway was the one I studied very, very closely. He made it look so easy. There's a lot of white space on his page with all dialogue. He relied on dialogue and didn't describe people physically in detail, yet you knew them. That is one of my rules. Describe very briefly. One of my other favorites, a great influence on me, was Richard Bissell. He wrote *Seven and a Half Cents* which became *Pajama Game*. And Mark Harris, particularly *Bang the Drum Slowly*. Let's see. I read Earl Stanley Gardner's *Donald Lamb* and *Bertha Cool* novels. I liked them and I liked Frederick Brown, particularly *Screaming Mimi*.

What are your politics?
I vote Democratic more often than Republican. I vote for the individual not the party.

You're a Catholic.
I was brought up Catholic, went to Catholic schools through college. University of Detroit High School, a Jesuit school. Took Classics courses in Latin and Greek, four years of Latin, two years of Greek. I think I had a good education. The Jesuits teach you how to think.

You used to have a drinking problem.
Yes, a serious one. I entered AA in 1974. I was in AA for three years and then went to Morocco on a possible film project and began drinking again. I was away from my support. But I got back on the program again when I returned to the States. I remember at my first AA meeting I asked a guy if he didn't get bored at parties if he didn't drink and he answered, 'If you think you're going to get bored, why go?' I haven't had a drink since January 24, 1977 at 9:30 A.M.

You do smoke.
I've had three between ten and one today. That's not bad. Yesterday I only had eight all day. When I'm writing, when I'm stuck, I'll light up, but maybe half of it will burn in the ashtray.

What do you do to relax or stay in shape?
To stay in shape, I play tennis. To relax I watch nature shows and documentaries on television, and sometimes a movie.

Favorite movies?
Quite a few. I can watch *All That Jazz* any time. *The Long Good Friday*. Maybe my all-time favorite is *Quest For Fire*. It's full of firsts. First joke, first frontal sex, a crazy movie.

What about Westerns, adventure movies?
The Plainsman, Charge of the Light Brigade, Lives of a Bengal Lancer, Captain Blood. I used to go to the theater when I was a kid and see those movies and then come home and sit on the front stoop and tell the stories to my friends. I guess that was my first venture into storytelling.

I don't see any pets around.
There aren't any. My former wife Joan and I had a little Lhasa apso named Emma who died when she was thirteen.

But you write about dogs.
Actually, I'm writing a children's book now. I don't know if it's going to work. My agent in Hollywood says that whenever I have an animal in one of my books I write something from the animal's point of view.

Like the gator in Maximum Bob?
Right. Well my agent thinks I should do a book from an animal's point of view.

It's getting late and I can see that Dutch is glancing at his yellow pad. He has pages left to do before the day ends.

We wander through the house to a small, neat room with lined bookshelves. He goes to one shelf and pulls down copies of old pulp magazines and paperbacks. They are Westerns with men firing guns at each other on the covers and each book and magazine bears the name Elmore Leonard.

They are well cared for, crisp of color. There is something almost magical in holding each of them.

Dutch returns the books and magazines to the shelves and looks around. This is his life's work, and it is clear that he is pleased with what he has done.

Ten Rules for Writing
By Elmore Leonard

These are rules I've picked up along the way to help me remain invisible when I'm writing a book, to help me show rather than tell what's taking place in the story. If you have a facility for language and imagery and the sound of your voice pleases you, invisibility is not what you are after then you can skip the rules. Still, you might want to look them over.

Never open a book with weather.

If it's only to create atmosphere and not a character's reaction to the weather, you don't want to go on too long. The reader is apt to leaf ahead looking for people. There are exceptions. If you happen to be Barry Lopez who has more ways to describe ice and snow than an Eskimo, you can do all the weather reporting you want.

Avoid prologues.

They can be annoying, especially a prologue following an introduction that comes after a foreword. But these are ordinarily found in nonfiction. A prologue in a novel is backstory, and you can drop it in anywhere you want.

There is a prologue in John Steinbeck's *Sweet Thursday*, but it's okay because a character in the book makes the point of what my rules are all about. He says, "I like a lot of talk in a book and I don't like to have nobody tell me what the guy who's talking looks like. I want to figure out what he looks like from the way he talks . . . figure out what the guy's thinking from what he says. I like some description but not too much of that. . . . Sometimes I want a book to break loose with a bunch of hooptedoodle. . . . Spin up some pretty words maybe or sing a little song with language. That's nice but I wish it was set aside so I don't have to read it. I don't want hooptedoodle to get mixed up with the story."

Never use a verb other than "said" to carry dialogue.

The line of dialogue belongs to the character, the verb is the writer sticking his nose in. But said is far less intrusive than grumbled, gasped, cautioned, lied. I once noticed Mary McCarthy ending a line of dialogue with "she asserted" and had to stop reading to get a dictionary.

Never use an adverb to modify the verb "said."

He admonished gravely. To use an adverb this way (or almost any way) is a mortal sin. The writer is now exposing himself in earnest, using a word that distracts and can interrupt the rhythm of the exchange. I have a character in one of my books tell how she used to write the historical romances "filled with rape and adverbs."

Keep your exclamation points under control.

You are allowed no more than two or three per 100,000 words of prose. If you have the knack of playing with exclaimers the way Tom Wolfe does, you can throw them in by the handful.

Never use the words "suddenly" or "all hell broke loose."

This rule doesn't require an explanation. I have noticed that writers who use "suddenly" tend to exercise less control in the application of exclamation points.

Use regional dialect, patois, sparingly.

Once you start spelling words in dialogue phonetically and loading the page with apostrophes, you won't be able to stop. Notice the way Anne Piroux captures the flavor of Wyoming voices in her book of short stories *Close Range*.

Avoid detailed descriptions of characters.

Which Steinbeck covered in Ernest Hemingway's *Hills Like White Elephants*: what do the "American and the girl with him" look like? "She had taken off her hat and put it on the table." That's the only reference to physical description in the story, and yet we see the couple and know them by their tones of voice with not one adverb in sight.

Don't go into great detail describing places and things.

Unless you're Margaret Atwood and can paint scenes with language or write landscapes in the style of Jim Harrison. But even if you're good at it, you don't want descriptions that bring the action, the flow of the story, to a standstill.

And finally:

Try to leave out the part that readers tend to skip.

A rule that came to mind in 1983. Think of what you skip reading a novel: thick paragraphs of prose you can see too many words in them. What the writer is doing, he's writing, perpetrating hooptedoodle, perhaps taking another shot at the weather, or has gone into the character's head, and the reader either knows what the guy's thinking or doesn't care. I'll bet you don't skip dialogue.

My most important rule is one that sums up 10:

If it sounds like writing, I rewrite.

Or, if proper usage gets in the way, it may have to go. I can't allow what we learned in English composition to disrupt the sound and rhythm of the narrative. It's my attempt to remain invisible, not distract the reader from the story with obvious writing. (Joseph Conrad said something about words getting in the way of what you want to say). If I write in scenes and always from the point of view of a particular character—the one whose view best brings the scene to life—I'm able to concentrate on the voices of the characters telling you who they are and how they feel about what they see and what's going on and I'm nowhere in sight.

What Steinbeck did in *Sweet Thursday* was title his chapters as an indication, though obscure, of what they cover. "Whom the Gods Love they Drive Nuts" is one. "Lousy Wednesday" another. The third chapter is titled "Hooptedoodle 1" and the 38th chapter "Hooptedoodle 2" as warnings to the reader, as if Steinbeck is saying, "Here's where you'll see me taking flights of fancy with my writing, and it won't get in the way of the story. Skip them if you want."

Sweet Thursday came out in 1954 when I was just beginning to get published, and I've never forgotten that prologue.

Did I read the hooptedoodles? Every word.

DONALD WESTLAKE

John Dortmunder was a man on whom the sun shone only when he needed darkness.
—*Bad News* by Donald Westlake

Donald Westlake lives in upstate New York, about an hour's ride outside of New York City by commuter train. I am the only one getting off at the stop at ten on a weekday morning, and he is the only one on the platform waiting.

He looks lean and fit. He recently fought a life-threatening bout with Lyme Disease which stopped his writing for almost a month. When he recovered, however, he was back at work with a vengeance, producing four books in the past two years.

We drive past rolling hills to a modest country house on a low hill. Don's wife Abby says 'hi' and goes on working with a man helping her with a stone garden wall.

Inside the house Don takes off his wide-brimmed hat, and we move into his office. A large nearly finished jigsaw puzzle sits on a table next to his desk.

"You do jigsaw puzzles to relax?"

"Yeah, and carpentry. My neighbor Walter and I built that barn across the road."

Through the window I see the barn.

"I'm impressed."

"We also built that gazebo. There's a stream back there with a drop off. We built the gazebo over the drop off. I'm not sure how we did it."

I can see a grassy slope a few dozen yards from the house and a pond at the bottom of the slope. A cat is slowly walking around the rim of the pond.

"We have two cats," says Don. "Barnaby and Betsy. That's Betsy. Barnaby wanderers away during the day."

We walk out to look at the pond and sit on a bench looking down at it with the rolling hills behind us. The faint mooing of cows is audible.

"We've run into each other at conferences all over the world," I say. "Is traveling part of your relaxation?"

"Well, I travel more than I want to. Abby loves to travel, and she plans fun trips. I think most writers, including me, would rather be at the desk writing than traveling. Larry Block is the one exception I know."

"Where did you grow up?"

"Albany, New York," he says. "Three of my four grandparents were born in Ireland. My father's father was from a line of Westlakes who had already been here. Westlakes, Pound, Fitzgeralds. All my grandparents were part of an immigration of Irish to different parts of New York."

"Irish Catholic?"

"All of them," he says as we head back to the house. "I went to Catholic schools and a Catholic church. I was born during the Depression. My father was always scrambling to make a living. He didn't go to college and he had a weird personality which I inherited. It served him badly but worked out for me as a writer."

We settle in the living room.

"My father had lots of jobs," says Don. "He was a real estate salesman, a bookkeeper and there was a time, about six months when he was a food broker, the middle man between the food companies, juice companies, fish canneries and the groceries and supermarkets. Every time he got a job the same thing happened. My father would get intensely interested in something about the job—intensity and no pleasure."

"For instance?"

"When he was a food broker, he got interested in tuna, wanted to know everything about tuna, though he didn't have to. The tuna was already in a can. All he had to do was sell the cans, but he became obsessed by tuna. I remember him taking me to a fish company to see a twenty-five minute movie about tuna fishing. He'd get totally absorbed with whatever it was, like tuna, and then suddenly get bored. He'd get indifferent to his job, sloppy and get fired."

"Every time?"

"Yeah. He did the same thing when he became a bookkeeper for Domino Sugar, had to learn everything about the sugar trade. Great worker for five months and then . . . fired."

"Did he ever hold onto a job?"

"He died during his last job. He was working for the State of New York. There was a tax on trucks depending on their unladen weight and how much they would carry. The laws were very confusing. My father's job was to drive around the state explaining the law to trucking companies."

"And he became obsessed with. . .?"

"Tax law, road use, what truckers are carrying. He had a heart attack and died before he lost interest."

"And this trait has helped you as a writer?"

"I get fascinated by what I'm writing, totally absorbed, and by the time I'm finished, I'm bored. But I'm a writer, so I don't have to stay there. I can just drop my interest in casinos, banks, DNA, prison systems, whatever."

"How did you get interested in carpentry?"

"My father's father was a carpenter, very good detail work, one of those taciturn Irishmen. I doubt if anyone under the age of twenty ever heard a word from his mouth. The only way he could express himself was by making little chairs, sometimes rocking chairs, for his grandchildren with their names carved on the backs. I had one."

"What about your mother's father?"

"Apparently a rowdy and a drunk. I only saw him once when I was nine or ten even though he lived in Albany. We were driving down Pearl Street, bad neighborhood at the time. There was this guy who looked like W.C. Fields sitting on a kitchen chair tilted back against a brick wall reading a newspaper. He was wearing a black suit and a white shirt. My dad said to my mother, 'There's your father' and my mother answered, 'Not in front of the children.'"

"Were you a reader when you were a kid?"

"Self-taught," he says. "I started reading when I was about three. When I was old enough to go to the library I was assigned to the children's book ghetto, kids books. But there were two

librarians who got to know me and freed me to take whatever books I wanted. I learned that censorship for children is absurd. If you're not ready for it, you don't absorb it. So when I was eight or nine years old I'd pick up a book on sexual pathology and be bored and move on to a pirate story. My reading was eclectic."

When he was a teen, Don went through one of his obsessive stages. He devoured everything by and about Erle Stanley Gardner.

"My father used to drive nuns from our church around the city. One day he was driving them and I gave him a book to return to the library, Gardner's *The Case of the Impatient Virgin*. One of the nun's saw the title. My father was obviously embarrassed."

"Any other writers get to you in the same way? Influence you?"

"Hammett," he said. "And much later Nabokov."

Don went to Champlain College in Plattsburg, New York for a year and a half until it was converted to a Strategic Air Command base. He returned to Albany, got a day job and went to Russell Sage College at night and then went into the Air Force in 1955.

"What did you do in the Air Force?"

"Orderly room clerk at the Ramstein Air Force Base in Germany. That's where my signature disappeared. I was the guy who had to sign everything."

After the Air Force, Don enrolled at Binghamton College on the GI Bill.

"I went a total of four years to college, interrupted by a stint in the Air Force," he says. "I never got a degree. I did get married."

Don's first wife was an actress.

"She was good," he says, "but her problem was the thickness of her skin. About ninety-eight percent of an actor's life is rejection. We moved to New York so she could look for work. By then I knew I was going to be a writer and it didn't matter where I lived as long as I could get to a post office."

While his wife took acting classes and looked for work, Don got a job with the Scott Meredith Literary Agency as a reader. He held the job six months.

"It was like boot camp," he says. "By the end of it, I understood the publishing world in New York the way I had learned to understand the Air Force."

Abby comes in from the garden, takes off her wide-brimmed hat and we sit down to a leisurely lunch, talk a little about work being done on the property and the trip the Westlakes are about to take to England and France.

I ask about their children.

"Abby and I have seven," Don says. "We have none together. It's complicated. My first wife and I had two sons, Sean and Steven. Sean is a carpenter. He lives in Upstate New York about an hour from here. He and his wife have a little girl. Steven works on Wall Street. He's divorced and has a twelve-year-old daughter. After my first marriage, I married a widow with one son. Her husband had died of leukemia when he was twenty-eight. I adopted her son and he took the name Westlake. He lives in Iowa City and manages a store. My second wife and I had one son, Paul, who lives in Brooklyn. He's a pianist, a composer, a short story writer. He's worked in the perfume business and as a grip on non-union movies."

I also learn that one of Abby's three children, her oldest girl, Adrian Heidi, is a private chef. Patrick is a chef too and has a son, and Katharine hasn't decided what she's going to do with her life. At the moment, she's a substitute teacher.

After lunch, Don and I return to the living room and I ask him what the first thing he ever published was.

"A gimmick science fiction story for a magazine called *Universe* that lasted two issues after they published my story. I got thirty dollars. My second story was also science fiction. I got twenty dollars for that one and then, for the third, I got $150 from *Rogue Magazine*."

"So now," I say, "you've written over a hundred published novels under a dozen different names—three of them female—and have two of the most successful mystery series in history going, the Dortmunder novels and the Parker novels. Many of them have been made into

movies with some interesting casting. Parker has been played by Robert Duvall in *The Outfit*, Jim Brown in *The Split*, Lee Marvin in *Point Blank*, Peter Coyote in *Slayground*, and Mel Gibson in *Payback*. Did you ever have an actor in mind to play Parker?"

"A younger Jack Palance. I definitely had Jack Palance in mind when I wrote the first Parker novel, big, strong, dangerous, cat-like and quick. Even without trying he carries a menace in his voice, even when he's trying to be funny. I saw the Jack Palance who was in *Panic in the Streets*."

"Dortmunder," I say. "When I read the books, I always imagine you as Dortmunder. Dortmunder's been played by actors ranging from Robert Redford and George C. Scott to Martin Lawrence. Did you have someone in mind?"

"That's funny," says Don with a laugh, "but I see my neighbor Walter as Dortmunder. He's perfect even though I didn't meet Walter until 1980. The odd thing now is that I have to keep from writing Walter when I write a Dortmunder."

Don is also a screenwriter, a member of the Board of Directors of the Writers Guild of America, East. His most notable film scripts were *The Stepfather*, which spawned an extremely successful series of sequels, and *The Grifters*, for which he received an Academy Award nomination for best screenplay.

"With screenplays," he says, "it's sometimes helpful to have an actor in mind, but I just couldn't figure out the mother. I had no trouble visualizing the son and the girlfriend and when it was cast, John Cusack and Annette Bening were a near perfect fit, but I couldn't get the mother in my mind so I couldn't get her on the page."

Don met with the director, Stephen Frears who said he was going to talk to Cher and Angelica Huston about playing the mother.

"Angelica turned it down," says Don. "Then I got a call saying they had hired Melanie Griffith. I used a word I've never used in dialogue or speech. She's not right for the part. As it turned out, Melanie agreed with me and quit the project. Stephen went back to Anjelica who reluctantly said 'yes.'"

"How about some quick Q&A's?" I ask.

Don nods.

Kaminsky: You see a lot of movies. Do you have an all-time favorite?
Westlake: *The Treasure of the Sierra Madre*, followed by *Dr. Strangelove* and *Bringing Up Baby*. *Groundhog Day* is definitely a keeper. Forty years from now they'll be talking about *Groundhog Day*.

Is Bogart your favorite actor?
Bogart could only do a couple of things, but boy could he do them well. I'd say Alec Guinness might be my favorite. He could do anything.

Favorite author?
Anthony Cole. I just read *Dancing to the Music in Time* again.

What do you look for in a book?
Abby and I agree that in fiction we like characters who can read and write, who have some wit and can't be mistaken for their mules. So, no more Faulkner for a while.

Do you listen to music when you write?
Jazz, older jazz, swing era, up to Coltrane.

What's your least favorite part about being a writer?
The discussion after the first draft of a screenplay. Being a novelist involves making forty-seven decisions a page. Being a screenwriter you have to remember why you made those decisions and justify them.

Your favorite part about being a writer?
Writing. I don't outline. I don't know what's going to happen next. The fun part is telling myself the story.

I've been on panels with you, and you have an extremely funny deadpan wit. You do smile and laugh but there is a serious look about you. The happiest look I've seen on you was when you showed me the pond earlier. Do people read you the wrong way?

They tend to think I'm more friendly and outgoing than I think I am.

Politics?

Haunted, more liberal than not. I almost never touch politics in my writing but one of my books did have a political aura about it. I dedicated it to my friend Mickey Swerner, one of the three young men killed in Mississippi during the move to register black voters.

Goodman, Chaney, Swerner? Mississippi Burning?

Yes. Mickey and I were in the same weekly poker game. I thought he was apolitical. The only political thing I ever heard him say was, "It's the same old story, The Moochers vs. The Misers." I had never heard the American political system described that way.

Are you a practicing Catholic?
I gave that up in my teens, but I may be the only ex-Catholic you will ever meet who is not anti-Catholic. Ex-Catholics tend to carry a grudge.

Any fears?
Not really. For many years I had a low-level fear of not being able to continue to make a living as a writer. That fear has finally gone away, but I lived with it for thirty years.

How long did it take you to sell your first novel?
Well, I did a few little paperbacks, short books, but I don't count them as first books. They're full of bad habits.

Such as?
Every chapter had to be twenty pages long and the whole book had to be ten chapters. Then I wrote one I considered to be my real first novel. I showed it to my agent who pointed out I was still doing the mechanical stuff. So I rewrote it, and the agency said they'd sell it as a paperback. I said no. Simon and Schuster hated it, but an editor at Random House liked it but wanted me to make some changes. I rewrote it again and they published it.

It was called . . .
The Mercenary. I got $1,000 for it.

If you weren't a writer, what would you be?
A farm hand or a stock boy in a supermarket. I have no marketable skills.

Last question. My daughter's question. If you could have only one super power, what would it be?
To fly, but I've got to be invisible so I won't get shot down.

FAYE AND JONATHAN KELLERMAN

"We believe that God—whom we call Hashem, which means 'the name' in Hebrew—is the source of all matter and neither a creation nor susceptible to destruction. Hashem just is. God is material and God is spiritual. And He described His heaven as a limitless way before science got into the act."
—*Jupiter's Bones* by Faye Kellerman

". . . my personal favorite, old lady smothered in her bed back when Nixon was President. Should've gotten my degree in ancient history."
    "English lit's not a bad fit either."
    "How so?"
    "Everyone's got a story," I said.
    "Yeah, but once I'm listening to them, you can forget happy endings."
—*Flesh and Blood* by Jonathan Kellerman

Faye and Jonathan Kellerman live in a spacious house on Sunset Boulevard in Los Angeles. In all the years I've worked in and visited Los Angeles, I've passed their house dozens, maybe hundreds of times but didn't see it because the house is low and surrounded by tall bushes. The driveway of the house is gated. I've called ahead and Faye is waiting for me at the front door when I arrive.

As we enter the house I am struck by the openness of its design. My attention is immediately drawn to the many and varied paintings along the walls and up the stairway to my left.

"We collect art, much of it by Jonathan," Faye says leading me into a breakfast room where we sit down for coffee.

I'm told Jonathan is on the way.

Before we start talking over coffee, three girls around ten years old come in laughing and I am introduced to Aliza, the youngest of the Kellermans' four children. Faye urges Aliza and her friends to get something to eat; the girls agree and disappear.

I hear Jonathan come in from somewhere near the kitchen behind us, greet the girls and join us at the table.

"She's a lot of fun," Jonathan says sitting. "Aliza means 'happy' in Hebrew, and she lives up to her name. Brilliant, loves to write, draw. The kids are great—a varied bunch, all distinctive personalities. I think they show the results of having a great mother."

"The other kids are. . .?" I ask.

"Jesse," says Jonathan, "is heavily involved in theater and is rewriting what I think is a very good novel. If I'm known for anything, at some point I'll be known as Jesse Kellerman's dad.

"Our oldest is Rachel. She's graduating from the University of Pennsylvania, majoring in psychology. She's trying to decide whether she wants to be a psychologist like her father."

"And our second daughter Illana," Faye says, "is a vocal prodigy. She has a three-and-a-half

octave range. By the time she was sixteen, she had recorded, done some acting, and voice-overs for Nickelodeon and Schoolhouse Rock."

Jonathan adds, "An excellent student. Editor of her school newspaper, a really good journalist."

"What were your families like, grandparents, parents, brothers, sisters?"

Faye says her father was born in a town in Poland that is now part of the Ukraine, the part known as The Pale to which Jews were confined.

"My grandfather on my mother's side was born in Odessa," she says. "His last name was Marner, which means little mole in German. My mother's parents didn't go through Ellis Island. They went directly to St. Louis where they had relatives. That's where my mother was born and where she met my father. They lived in St. Louis until 1957, when I was four. My father had a butcher shop. They moved west because they hated the cold winters."

Faye has two older brothers, one of whom was an actuary and a computer expert. He now lives in Jerusalem. The other brother is a meteorologist who lives nearby with Faye's mother.

"Your family moved directly to California in 1957?"

"No, to Tucson. They made the mistake of going in July. A few days later we were on our way to Los Angeles, the Valley, Sherman Oaks. My father opened a kosher deli in the Los Feliz district of Los Angeles, not a particularly affluent neighborhood at the time, but he got friendly with quite a few B movie stars."

"Like?"

"The Three Stooges."

"As Adam Sandler says in his song," I say, "all Three Stooges are Jewish."

"Trouble was," says Faye, "the neighborhood at the time couldn't support a Jewish deli so my father took a job for two years and then opened a Jewish bakery. I used to help when I could. I loved the smell of fresh bread."

"And then?"

"My father died when he was fifty-three. My mother tried to run the bakery and failed. Fortunately, my brothers and I were able to take care of her. By that time I had been married to Jonathan for two years and finishing dental school at U.C.L.A. It took me a long time to recover from my father's death."

"You're a dentist?"

"Yes, but I never practiced," she says. "By the time I passed my boards, I had a baby and Jonathan wasn't all that established. And I wanted to be a full-time mother."

It was then that Faye began to write.

"Jonathan was a great inspiration, the first writer in the family. He was the reason I started to write and my main encouragement when I did write. He still is."

A dog barks from somewhere in the back of the house.

"We have three dogs," says Jonathan.

"The yappy one is Dreamy," says Faye. "A papillon. We also have a fish pond in the yard and a salt water aquarium."

"And your family?" I say turning to Jonathan.

"My parents were born in America, both of them. My dad's from the Bronx. My mom's from the Lower East Side of Manhattan. My dad's parents came to America in 1902 from Romania, not far from Odessa. They came after my great-grandfather died in a fall at the age of ninety-eight and my great-grandmother was murdered, probably by some nationalist anti-Semitic group. My grandfather drifted from one thing to another. He owned a store, invested in the stock market, lost all his money, worked as a brakeman on the railroad. He ended up owning a music store, and my dad got interested in electronics. You know, those Victrolas with horns, wax cylinder recordings? My dad became a self-taught electronics prodigy. When World War II came, he was given an IQ test and scored so high that he was sent to work on developing the atomic bomb in Washington."

Then Jonathan's father signed a petition, an anti-war petition. He lost his security clearance, got drafted and found himself spending three-and-a-half years in Europe, including being part of the Battle of the Bulge. When the war ended, he went back to the Bronx, got a job with RCA and married Jonathan's mother. They met on the Staten Island ferry.

"My dad was one of the pioneers in creating television," says Jonathan. "He went to work for another company and invented a capacitor that earned his company five million dollars. In 1959, after running his own business out of a basement in Queens, we moved from our GI Bill home to California where my father started a successful electronics business my brother still runs."

"Your mother?"

"She was a semi-professional and a model," he says. "She was on television as a dancer in the 1950's. She had gone to high school with Zero Mostel and they remained friends. My mother was part of a dance group. Their accompanist was John Cage."

"You have a brother and sister?"

"Both younger," he says. "My sister lives in Beverly Hills. She's married to a psychiatrist. My brother has a degree in engineering from Columbia. He's the one who runs the electronics company. We call him The Tycoon."

It was time for lunch. We go to the Kellermans' favorite kosher deli where they are both warmly greeted. The food is great and plentiful and the deli, less noisy than one might expect from the full tables and booths. I ask Faye and Jonathan about religion.

"My dad's family was not religious," he says. "But my mother's family was Hasidic, very religious. I went to Jewish schools through a Yeshiva high school. Then I went to U.C.L.A. where I was a psychology major."

"My family went to an orthodox synagogue, kept kosher, but we went to public school," says Faye.

"So you belong to an orthodox congregation?"

"Three of them," says Jonathan.

"Three modern orthodox congregations," says Faye.

"Just to be supportive," he says.

"Religion plays a very important part in our lives," says Faye, "and is an important part of my writing. It doesn't appear in Jonathan's books at all."

"And it resonates with me," I say. "I was reading one of your books in bed about a year ago and your character Rena said something about never putting anything on top of the Holy Scriptures. I realized I had an Anne Perry novel on top of the Bible next to my side of the bed. I took it off, and I've been careful not to repeat that mistake again."

"I chose to write about religious characters to add a dimension to the mystery," she says. "It was a life I was intimately involved in, and I knew people really didn't understand what it meant to be a religious Jew, a practicing Jew."

"There are moments, characters in your books who touch on religion," I say to Jonathan. "For example, in *Billy Straight*, Billy finds refuge in a synagogue with an old Jewish man who befriends him when he most needs a friend, but generally religion plays no strong role in your work."

"In my life, yes," he says. "I'm a Jew, a Zionist."

"With Jonathan's first Alex Delaware book, *When the Bough Breaks*," says Faye, "the publisher wanted to set up book signings on Friday nights and Saturdays, supposedly the best times for signings. Jonathan wouldn't break the Sabbath. He got a lot of grief."

"A few years ago," I say to Faye, "I tried to get you to come to Sarasota for a book fair. You couldn't do it because you'd have had to travel on a Friday night or a Saturday."

"But it wasn't religion that drove me as a writer. The thing that drove me was my experience as a psychologist focusing on family psychopathology," Jonathan says. "I had been writing since I was nine. I always won the essay contests. When I went to U.C.L.A. I worked as a cartoonist for the school newspaper, wrote news articles, had a column. I wrote through graduate school, and when I was a practicing psychologist. I wrote a lot of bad books—eight or nine of them— that never got published."

"What was wrong with those first novels?"

"I didn't have enough life experience," he says. "Working in an inner city hospital exposed me to some really strong stuff. And then I found my voice."

"Found your voice?"

"Yes, I read Ross MacDonald's *The Underground Man*. Then I read all of his books and recognized there was a genre of Southern California hardboiled writing. So I read Chandler, Horace McCoy, David Goodis, Jonathan Lattimer and James M. Cain. I just didn't find writing about religion that interesting to me. It's interesting to Faye, but it's the psychological aspects of living in Southern California that get to me, dealing with family psychology gone really bad."

"What part of that psychology most interested you?"

"The fact that you can't escape the past, present and future. Family. That's what my books are about."

"But that's what your books are about, too," I say to Faye. "Family."

"I have no choice but to deal with family," she says. "The family life in my books is at the core. If I have a plot in which Rena is put in the background a little, the book becomes a Peter Decker police procedural. My readers don't like it."

Jonathan added, "I think Faye deals with families as well as any writer and better than most. She writes from experience and she has tremendous sensitivity and understanding for people of all ages. She gets the teenagers just right. She has a golden ear for dialogue."

"You said you were a cartoonist in college," I say. "I've seen your work and your paintings in your house. I think you're very, very good. Why didn't you pursue this?"

Jonathan says, "I still paint, still do cartoons for fun."

I ask him if he will do one for me, and he quickly and effortlessly does a cartoon drawing of himself and Faye and hands it to me.

"I did a caricature in 1967," he says. "Bobby Kennedy. Big head, small body, not too complimentary. Cartoons aren't meant to be. Somebody suggested I send it to William Buckley at the *National Review*. Buckley's sister Priscilla, the managing editor, said they wanted to use it on the cover. Before it went to press, Bobby Kennedy was assassinated. Of course they pulled it. One of life's twists. I might have wound up a political cartoonist."

We return to the Kellerman house where I'm shown two offices separated by several rooms including the large living room. Both their offices are neat, lots of dark wood—the offices of writers.

"When you finish a book," I ask, "do you show it to each other?"

"We used to show each other our work chapter by chapter as we wrote," he says. "But we're more self-confident now. Still, it's like having a two-person writers' group. If I have a question, I ask Faye. Generally, though, we like to write by ourselves."

"We tend to point out the major things," she says. "Like bringing in a character the other person thought had been mentioned before but really hadn't."

"Right," he says, "we'll point out things like that, things we've left out because we're writing too fast."

"How fast do you write?"

"I do about five or six pages a day after I rewrite what I have done the day before," he says.

"Every hundred pages or so I go back and do another rewrite. I do a lot of rewriting, but I don't want to get too obsessed and bogged down. I always try to press ahead."

"When I write," adds Faye, "I write the novel straight through. I work from a detailed outline. Some of my outlines are so complete that I can just lift a chapter from the outline and paste it onto the novel with a little bit of cleaning up. I've even written out of order when something particularly strikes me or I know I have a certain scene coming up in the outline and I'm in the mood to write it."

"You're the only writer I know who does that," I say.

"It takes a certain kind of brilliant mind to be able to do that," says Jonathan. "I write linear, follow the plot, step by step."

"How many pages a day do you do?" I ask Faye.

"Anywhere from three to fifteen. I try to finish two chapters a week."

"My record," says Jonathan, "is twenty-two pages in a day. I think we treat writing as a job, a fun job, but a job that has to get done."

Jonathan offers to show me his guitar collection while Faye stays in the house. We move into a small garden behind the house. I follow him up the steps into a neatly painted white wooden building. The lights come on, and we're in a bright room filled with perfectly polished guitars, neatly displayed, but this is not simply a museum. Jonathan can and does play every instrument here.

I admire a smooth, mahogany guitar on the shelf. He takes it down and begins to play, his face serious, his fingers moving swiftly on a Flamenco piece that resonates. It is beautiful.

"Thank you," I say.

He nods and smiles.

"You have a favorite guitarist?"

"Stevie Ray Vaughn," he says putting the guitar back carefully. "Probably the best blues guitarist, best pop guitarist ever. He died in a helicopter crash about ten years ago."

Back in the house, I ask them both what kind of music they like.

"Jazz," says Jonathan immediately. "Old stuff. Sonny Rollins, Benny Goodman, almost any jazz guitar. I like bluegrass, country music, rock, even a little rap and I'm definitely open to classical. I'm open to any music if I think it's good."

"I used to say I like everything but polkas," says Faye. "I grew up with show tunes, because my mother played piano by ear and loved the Broadway shows of the 40's and 50's. Rodgers and Hammerstein, Rodgers and Hart, Lerner and Lowe, Jerome Kern. I do listen to pop music today because of the kids. And I like country—though I think a lot of it is sappy—but the musicianship is the best. Nobody plays like country musicians, but I do get tired of hearing about old grandma and the pickup truck and the barbecue sauce on the T-shirt. I also love bluegrass and classical music."

"You play an instrument?"

"Violin."

"Our musical taste is really eclectic," says Jonathan. "Last Saturday night we went to a bluegrass concert. The week before we went to a Hawaiian slack key guitar concert. This Saturday we're going to a jazz concert."

"Music, painting, writing," I say. "What do you think is the source of creativity?"

"I don't think there's one source," says Faye, "but ultimately, being a religious person, I think the source of creativity is God."

"I think," adds Jonathan, "creativity is probably inborn. Brain chemistry and environment brings it out. It's hard to kill it, even in a bad family. Children are more creative than adults. I've done hypnosis, and children are much better at it than adults, because hypnosis is fantasy. Really creative writers are people who never quite lost some of that childish thinking. The important thing for a parent to do is not to kill it. If you ask one kid what he would do if you gave him a broom, he might say he'd sweep the floor. Ask another kid and he might say, 'I'd fly.' Don't make fun of the second kid. I was always the kid who got in trouble in school for spacing out in class and daydreaming, fantasizing. Creative people are all like that."

"I'm worse," I say. "I actually failed two grades because I dreamed through them. I was probably the best read kid in both of those grades, but I sat in science class making up stories. I made up the two grades but I have never stopped day dreaming."

"So many dreams and stories," says Jonathan. "So little time. I have outlines for fourteen books I want to write."

"Your ideas just come to you," I said. "But what do you say to people who ask you where those ideas come from?"

"I know some writers give a flip answer," says Jonathan, "but it's a reasonable question. I get my ideas from a wide variety of sources. Sometimes it comes from a character; sometimes it's an event or a snippet of dialogue. Usually the idea for a book is the culmination of things I've been thinking about for years. For example, I'd been thinking a long time about gothic novels, *Jane Eyre*, *Wuthering Heights*, a frightened girl in a big house."

"*Private Eyes*," I say.

"Yes, that was my gothic novel, but whatever the book is, it's a combination of thoughts I've been thinking, notes I've been taking, people I meet, an experience I have or hear about."

"My answer is simple," says Faye. "Because the question is so overwhelming. I give a short answer, 'Everywhere and anywhere.'"

In the living room just off of Jonathan's office, they show me neat boxes and cases. Faye opens a case and takes out a scroll about two feet high. I recognize it. It's a Torah, the first five books of the Scriptures. I see the ones at my synagogue on the Sabbath and holy days. They come in different sizes and have different protective covers, but they all have one thing in common. They are carefully written in Hebrew by highly trained specialists, each letter of every word perfect and duplicating the lettering of the Torah before it. There is no going back to make corrections. Each letter must be right the first time. It can take years to complete a single one.

"People have misread the Bible throughout history," says Jonathan. "Bad translations. For example, the Bible does not say 'Thou Shalt Not Kill.' It says, 'Thou Shalt Not Murder.' Totally different word. It has no relevance to capital punishment."

"And 'Thou Shalt Not Steal' doesn't refer to robbery," says Faye carefully putting the Torah away. "It refers to kidnapping for ransom."

"And," Jonathan jumps in, "'An eye for an eye, a tooth for a tooth' means monetary compensation. It's clear. If you take someone's eye out, you pay them for it. Too many people see these and other sections of the Scriptures as being about revenge. They're about compensation."

"How about some quick Q&A's?" I ask.

They agree.

Kaminsky: Who do you write for?

Jonathan: Myself. I write so that when I read it the next day, I enjoy reading it.

Faye: I don't have a specific audience in mind, but I will go back and clean up some of the language, make some character less vile, change something if I think it will offend a certain group. I try to make my books as universal as possible.

Jonathan: I don't go out of my way to offend, but I don't pay attention to what people say. I'm astounded by my commercial success, eighteen bestsellers. Nobody wanted to publish *When the Bough Breaks*, because it was about child abuse. When I did get a publisher and a small advance, it was word of mouth that made it a bestseller.

Writer's block?

Faye: Don't have it.

Jonathan: Never have. Most people are not meant to be writers. It's like something you're born with, have a certain brain chemistry. Some people—you, Stephen King—can write a hundred books or more. Some people can write one or two good books. Then they say they have writer's block. Usually, the person has simply run out of what was in his or her well. Yes, there are people who really do clam up and freeze up. Anxiety, drug abuse, drinking, illness, stress, things that get in the way of doing any kind of work. It's not that the ideas aren't there.

Faye: I have situations where the writing comes easier and situations when it comes harder, but I force myself to write something. The most important thing is not to freeze when it's not perfect. Nothing is ever perfect. Don't be a baby and say 'It's not coming.' Work on it.

What's your favorite book of all you've written?
Faye: I can't name just one. *Past Sanctuary, Justice, Prayers for the Dead, The Forgotten* and *Stone Kiss.*
Jonathan: *When the Bough Breaks* has a special place in my heart because it was my first and I think it is really good, but I'd say *The Murder Book* is, at least so far, my favorite.

What are your favorite novels by other people?
Faye: *The Count of Monte Cristo, Double Indemnity, Over the Edge, When the Bough Breaks.*
Jonathan: I think you should exclude my books. It's going to look so sappy.
Faye: *When the Bough Breaks* reinvented the private eye novel.
Jonathan: I like *The Chill* and *The Count of Monte Cristo.*

All-time favorite movies?
Faye: *Double Indemnity* and *Casablanca.*
Jonathan: I'm a big Coen Brothers fan. I'd say *Fargo.*

What are your biggest fears?
Faye: I'm very good at burying my head in the sand. If there's a problem, I don't allow myself to think about it, to be afraid.
Jonathan: She's great at compartmentalizing. I'm not. I worked as a psychologist in a children's cancer ward for ten years. I handled it, but it was hard. Then fifteen years ago I had thyroid cancer. I was cured but it was a big slap in the face. Since then I've gotten more neurotic about mortality. I get the fear of death, but I'm not fear ridden.
Faye: In a small crisis, Jonathan gets very nervous, but in a big crisis, like when my father died, he was able to take care of me. In a big crisis, particularly a family crisis, he's fantastic, takes charge. In global crises, like 9/11 or what's happening in Israel, he is physically affected.
Jonathan: I think I may be a crime writer because of the Holocaust. I'm really aware of the rotten things people can think and do. I was in Israel in 1968, in the Jordan Valley. A shell fell fifty feet from where I was sleeping. I knew people who have been killed there. I became aware of a sense of threat. Until recently, Americans had an underdeveloped sense of threat.

Are there people you particularly admire?
Faye: The New Yorkers who stepped up to help each other, gave their lives to help others.
Jonathan: I admire Natan Sharansky, the current deputy prime minister of Israel, and John McCain. His dad was an admiral. He could have gotten out of going to Vietnam. He was captured and chose to stay in solitary confinement for years. He refused to be treated differently from other prisoners. That kind of standing up for principles is rare.

Do you speak any other languages?
Jonathan: Hebrew fluently.
Faye: French and Spanish if people speak slowly enough, and Hebrew if people speak really, really slow. I can handle myself in Hebrew while in Israel.

It's getting late, and I remind them that Jonathan was going to show me some of the art they have collected.

"We started off originally collecting WPA art from the 1930's," he says moving to a painting on the wall. "We have California impressionism, a lot of realism, some Latin American art."

We pause in front of a painting by Thomas Hart Benton.

"It looks like a hodgepodge of styles," he says, "but there's an emphasis on paint, not many etchings or drawings. I think that's because I'm a painter and I appreciate what goes into a painting."

The number of paintings and different styles is overwhelming. Jonathan has something to say about every painting, glossing over his own basically realistic works. His eyes scan each painting, stopping to focus on some aspect of a number of paintings as if he is noticing and admiring some detail for the first time.

"Were there painters or writers in either of your families?" I ask as we finish the tour.

Faye says "No."

But Jonathan says, "One of my great-great-grandfathers designed a lot of government buildings in Bucharest. My dad published poetry and sculpted."

Before walking out the door, I comment that they seem to be one of the most compatible couples I've ever met.

Jonathan says, "We have a really good, solid marriage and a really good romantic and working marriage. I put an emphasis on 'working' because nobody can be married thirty years without really working at it. There is a lot of compromise, compromise between artistic personalities, between raising the children, a lot of compromise on religious issues. There's nothing in life that we go through that hasn't involved compromise. The one thing we don't have to compromise on is our writing."

MARTIN CRUZ SMITH

Gulls burst over the Polar Star as if blown by light that rolled like a wind over the factory ship. Clouds lit. The windows of the trawlers flashed, and at last, out of the dark rose the low green shore of home.
—*Polar Star* by Martin Cruz Smith

It's raining as I drive down the two-lane road into Mill Valley in Marin County, California. Incongruously, in this upper middle class community surrounded by mountains, I pass a Moslem mosque where the American Taliban, John Walker Lindh, converted to Islam.

I meet Martin "Bill" Smith in town at a small stand-alone restaurant that's part Mexican, part remnant from the days when hippies lived in the valley.

The first thing Bill tells me when we're seated in a small colorfully decorated booth is that he has an appointment with an endodontist later to take care of a needed root canal.

"How do you feel about babysitting my granddaughter for a few hours?" he asks.

I tell him it's fine with me.

Over iced tea, I say, "First thing we should get straight is what I call you in this interview. Writers refer to you as Bill."

"That's my name, Martin William Wallace Smith," he says. "I've always been Bill to my friends; sometimes they call me Martin. When I first started writing, I found out there were several writers out there named William Smith. My mother was Mexican-Indian. I wanted something from that heritage recognized in my work so . . . Martin Cruz Smith."

"Since we're talking about names, let's talk about your family, your parents."

We've both ordered burritos. They're served quickly by a smiling waitress who clearly recognizes Bill as a frequent customer.

"My father's side of the family was very upper middle class in Reading, Pennsylvania," he says. "My grandfather was a gas company executive and a lay preacher in the Episcopal Church. His ancestors were English: Smiths. My grandmother was either English or French, depending on what day you asked her."

"And your father?"

"He was on the road to being an engineer, but he dropped out of school to become a jazz musician. He played the saxophone with a local black jazz band, usually at a brothel. In those days you could have white bands or black bands but not mixed race bands."

"What'd he do?"

"Put on a black face," says Bill. "He was a redhead, so I don't think he fooled anybody. They just pretended they didn't notice. He got into bebop early, played with Red Rodney's band in New York and around Philadelphia, but when he got married and I came along, he also had a steady day job with the Budd company in Philly working on parts for cars, tanks, railroad equipment."

"Where were you born?"

"Reading, grew up in Philly."

"How did your parents meet?"

"Music," he says. "My mother was a nightclub singer, a beautiful girl from New Mexico, part Mexican, part Pueblo Indian. She grew up on a reservation where her father—my grandfather—was a stone mason. My mother studied classical music at the University of New Mexico. She traveled to New York City to sing at something called the Festival of Gas. My father's dad had gotten my father a gig there. He was taken with her immediately and got her interested in jazz. She moved to New York to become a jazz and ballad singer—Cole Porter, Gershwin, Johnny Mercer. She was a headliner, particularly in Philly, for a long time."

We finish eating and decide to head for Bill's house. It's still raining. The road is narrow and gets narrower still when we turn onto a smaller road and start heading up a mountain.

"Are your parents retired?"

"Yes, well they're in their eighties," he says negotiating an ever-narrowing road that keeps going up and up. "After my mother stopped singing, she became an Indian rights director and activist and, with my dad, ran a Montessori school on a reservation."

"Are you named for anyone?"

"My Uncle Bill," he says. "He died in World War II. He was a P-40 pilot, shot down over China. My grandfather was also named Bill."

"Other aunts and uncles?"

"My father also had a sister, but my mother was one of twenty-one children. Her mother had four husbands."

"You must have a lot of cousins."

"Hundreds," he says.

And still we're climbing upward in the rain, the road growing even narrower.

"I spent a lot of time with my mother's family, my cousins, in New Mexico when I was a kid."

"You have a brother and sister, right?"

"Older brother, Jack, magazine writer. My sister is younger than I am. I'm the middle child. My sister Beatrice is a Montessori teacher."

"When did you move from Reading to Philadelphia?"

"When I was ten, I went to the Germantown Academy. My brother went there, too. I was on the debate team and wrestling team. My brother and I were both considered smart alecks, wise guys, pains in the ass."

It's still raining when we pull into the driveway of a huge house at the very top of the mountain.

"You were living in New York City before you moved here," I say. "Why here? Why move?"

"We had the two girls, and then Sam was born. We didn't want to raise kids in New York and have to tell them that Central Park was the woods. And we didn't want to worry about the kids, what taxi they were in, when did we see them last."

"But Mill Valley? You moved from New York City to the top of a mountain across the continent."

"I just came to California on my own, got in a rented car, and drove north from Los Angeles, stopping when I felt like it. I stopped in Mill Valley, liked it. So did my wife. So we bought this land and built this house."

The house is multi-leveled with breathtaking views in all directions.

"You designed the house?" I ask as we walk up a flight of steps.

"My wife and I," he says opening the door. "We wanted a house that looked like a small village, but since we're on a hill, we can't sprawl out."

The rooms in the house are all large, walls of wood, bookcases filled with books on the walls and even up the stairways. And vistas from every window.

"It's a good thing you're not afraid of heights."

"I am," he says. We are greeted by a large friendly dog introduced as Lucy.

"I never go near the edge of a mountain. It would take two strong men to get me anywhere near the precipice. I love open spaces. All the rooms in the house are large, open."

"But you fly a lot."

"I'm afraid of falling. Airplanes are actually claustrophobic."

It's at this point that I'm introduced to Bill's wife and year-old granddaughter. I'm invited to dinner and accept. Their daughter Mel and her husband will be joining us.

Bill's wife has been his editor since he left college. She also tutors English to Mexican and Central Americans in English and Spanish.

Bill's wife excuses herself to get some things ready for dinner before driving Bill to the dentist. Their granddaughter toddles around the warm, comfortable room.

"How did you and your wife meet?"

"First day at school at the University of Pennsylvania. We were assigned seats next to each other, a psychology lab. Her maiden name was Arnold, direct descendent of William Arnold, brother of Benedict Arnold. The other side of her family is Dutch. They settled in New Amsterdam in 1634."

"What did you study at Penn?"

"Sociology," he says. "But I dropped out, couldn't do the statistics. From that point on for a few years I was in and out of college till I became the sports editor of the *News of Delaware County*, outside of Philadelphia. I also did politics, obits and even restaurant reviews."

"That's when you became a writer?"

"I don't know why, but people around me always seemed to assume I was going to be a writer."

"You left the newspaper . . ."

"To become a Good Humor man," he says with a smile. "White uniform, cap, bell, truck, the whole thing."

"Why?"

"To make more money than I was making as a reporter," he says. "I wanted to save enough to go to Europe, and I did. I was the top Good Humor man in the Philadelphia area. They assigned me what they thought was the worst area, an all-black neighborhood across the Benjamin Franklin Bridge into Camden, New Jersey."

"Where did you go in Europe?"

"I went to Rome to get together with a girlfriend, but we broke up and I went to Spain."

"How's your Spanish?"

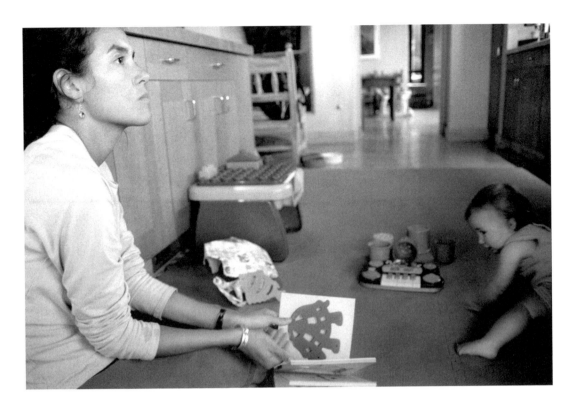

"I can still get by," he says checking his watch.

It's time to go to the dentist. I assure Bill and his wife that I can take care of fourteen-month-old Marcia, that I have had four children and changed hundreds of diapers. They put the baby in bed for a nap and I start browsing through books with Bill's dog at my side.

I notice a few familiar titles written by Bill. *Gorky Park*, being one of them. In 1981, Bill Smith created a new genre of mystery with that title, a modern tale featuring a protagonist from our then enemy, the Soviet Union. Arkady Renko made a hole in the Iron Curtain for millions of readers and showed them the humanity of those who were our supposed foes. In the process, Smith wrote a fascinating mystery about politics and national identity.

In five best-selling novels spanning twenty-three years, Arkady has been our guide to a dangerous world that Smith has made familiar through careful and accurate research and an understanding of people living in conditions far different from our own. In a sense, one common denominator in his novels is his ability to humanize people from other lands and other times.

A quick hour or so later, the Smiths are back and so is Marcia's mother Mel, the oldest of the Smith's three children. She has just moved back from New Mexico where she and her husband, a pediatrician, worked on a Navajo Reservation in public health at the Ship Rock Medical Center, Indian Health Services.

Both Mel and her sister Lucia went to Merritt College in Oakland. Lucia is a physician's assistant. Their brother Sam recently finished his undergraduate degree in film at New York University.

Bill says he is feeling no pain from his root canal and after dinner—it is still raining—we sit down next to the fireplace to talk about writing. I ask if he would mind a few quick questions and he agrees.

Kaminsky: You used other names on your work before you settled on your own name. Why?
Smith: I loved doing those early books, but I had an idea early on that I was going a step higher and I didn't want to carry the baggage of those early books with me.

So, you consider those early books inferior?
Yeah.

When did you decide to use your name?
The first time I decided to write well.

Which was when? Nightwing?
No, I wrote *Nightwing* to steal time and make a living while I worked on *Gorky Park*.

Let's talk about Gorky Park. You wrote it for Dutton, but they didn't want to publish it when you finished it?
No, they did want to publish it but they weren't enthusiastic. So I bought it back from them for the advance. It took me another two years to find a publisher who was enthusiastic. And it was all uphill from there.

Speaking of uphill, you said you run three miles four times a week. Up and down this mountain?
Yes, with Mel when she's here. If not, on my own.

You play a lot of music in your house. Do you listen to music when you write?
Not usually. I even pull down the shades so I won't be distracted from the page.

Given your parents' interest in jazz, I guess you listen to a lot of it.
Right. I listen to a lot of Ella and Louis, and I really like a young saxophonist named Mark Turner and Mark Redmon. I really like the ballads of Diana Krall.

What's the role of inspiration, if any, in your writing?
If you wait for inspiration, you're dead. You're at the ball park, suited up. You have to play.

You have a fixed schedule?
Nine to five. If I get a usable page and a half in that time, I'm happy. I might actually write ten pages, but by the time I finish with it, I'm down to that page and a half I'm satisfied with. Every page is written three or four times.

Are you an author or a writer?
I'm a writer. I don't think I've ever called myself an author. 'Author' sounds like something you did. 'Writer' sounds like something you do.

Do you write for yourself or the reader?
There's a point between me and the reader. I write up to that point and the reader listens. It's like jazz. Each story has a rhythm, each sentence, each paragraph, the entire book has to keep modulating going back and forth. I feel it.

Like jazz.
When I get into an impasse and I don't know what's supposed to happen next, I remember what Red Rodney told my father, "When in doubt, go back to the melody." When you begin the song or the novel, remember the tune you started out playing, go back to it and you'll know where you're supposed to be.

If there's so much improvising, and I agree that is what we do, how can you write an outline? Or do you?
I write outlines. I have to. I'm paid in advance. I write about nine pages.

I've heard that you have only spent ten days in Russia.
Two weeks. I did spend some time with Russians in the Bering Sea when I was doing the fishing book. I initially got into the Soviet Union through the Russian mystery writer, now dead, Julian Semyonov.

He wrote Petrovka 38. *I read that before I began my Russian novels. Then I met him.*
Quite a character, larger than life. He had me officially invited to Moscow and ran me around from a taping with the Minister of the Interior to a videotaping of me dancing with his daughter. He was very tight with the KGB and proud of it.

He wanted you to know he was working for the KGB but pretended that he wasn't. You challenge yourself in your writing. You've written books set in the Soviet Union, Rose *set in England a hundred years ago, and* December 6 *set in Japan. You plunge into Gypsy life and culture in 1970 in* Gypsy in Amber. *Don't you make it hard on yourself?*
What's hard is writing about something that doesn't interest me. I have to be an outsider to write. The outsider is not satisfied, the outsider can see what the eye can't see itself. The eye is the society of the world, the culture. It takes somebody who is outside it to some degree to see that and to describe it. Even the couple of times I've written about America, it's very much from the outside looking in. In *Stallion Gate*, my central character is doubly displaced, doubly an outsider. He leaves the Pueblo people and goes to New York and becomes a boxer, a musician and then as a soldier he returns home as an outsider.

You have a favorite author?
George Orwell. Great writer. Great influence on me.

In Rose*, you wrote about Wigan, the town in which Orwell set one of his stories, "The Road To Wigan Pier."*
Yes. One of his great works.

What is a great novel?
One that enlarges the person who reads it. A great novel changes a great number of people. To me, Margaret Wise Brown's *Goodnight Moon* and *The Runaway Bunny* are truly great books.

I know many people who say they don't read fiction.
Everything is fiction. Absolutely everything written, even the most factual book, is built on fiction. History is fiction, a mass of memories collected from faulty eyewitnesses.

Is there anyone in history you particularly admire?
Yes, the young man who stepped in front of that tank in Tiananmen Square in Beijing. I think what got me was the little white bag he was carrying. He was obviously just a very ordinary person doing something simple, extraordinary, pointed. There is sometimes something inside of a person, like that man, that makes the person simply do the right thing even if he knows he or she may be giving up life. It's not religious. Policemen and firemen often have it. That man in Tiananmen Square just calmly made that tank stop.

It is getting late. The rain is still falling, falling harder. After I say goodbye to the family, Bill drives me down the mountain.

When we say goodbye, I run into the bookstore next to where I parked my car. I have all of Bill Smith's novels, but I check to see how his books are doing in his hometown bookstore. They're sold out.

ROBERT B. PARKER

"John has warned me that you are a jokester. Well, I am not. If we are to have any kind of successful association, you'd best understand right now that I do not enjoy humor. Whether successful or not."

"Okay if now and then I enjoy a wry, inward smile if struck by one of life's vagaries?"
—*Looking for Rachel Wallace* by Robert B. Parker

The first time I met Bob Parker almost two decades ago, he was a gruff, burly man of average height with a knowing smile and a cocky, nervous confidence.

The man who greets me now at the door of his house in Cambridge, Massachusetts is definitely at ease, his smile sincere. The nervous, cocky man I knew has been replaced by a gentler, calmer man.

Across the street from the fourteen-room Parker house is the Harvard University graduate center, a tasteful white two-story building.

Bob and his wife Joan live a little over a block from Harvard's Loeb Theater where Joan, Bob says as we go into the house, is on the theater's board. Bob's office is immediately to the left as we go through the front door. His office is neat, comfortable, lined with shelves full of books. The room looks a little old-fashioned except for a Macintosh computer that sits on his desk, its monitor recessed and tilted up so that he can look down on it when he writes. His desk chair is next to the window facing the street. He looks out of it often as we talk.

"That's Pearl," Bob says, referring to a brown dog curled up on the sofa. "I've always had a dog named Pearl, all German shorthaired pointers."

"Susan Silverman's dog is also named—"

"Pearl," he says.

His eyes move to a photograph on the wall behind me of another dog.

"That was Ben, a Welsh corgi. I like dogs. So does Joan."

I notice a beat-up baseball glove on a shelf in front of the desk.

"Baseball," I say.

Any Parker fan knows from his books that the writer loves baseball in general and the Red Sox in particular. He looks at his glove wistfully and sits at his desk, hands folded behind his head.

"Baseball," he repeats. "I don't play anymore. I get my exercise from long walks with Joan. I don't run anymore because both knees are scoped. I still play some summer baseball. I'm a first baseman. I make up in width what I lack in height. It takes a lot for me to see the ball right. I don't start seeing it till the end of the season. I'm getting old and it's a bitch. I'm seventy years old and have gone through some major surgery. About two years ago, I had surgery to remove a pancreatic cyst. A vein ruptured and they almost lost me. "

"You look great," I say.

"Thanks, I feel good, lost thirty-five pounds. But age has crept up on me. I'm a very physical guy. I used to run ten miles a day and bench press three hundred pounds. I don't run now and I have a bad shoulder."

He looks at the baseball glove, gets up from his chair and motions for me to follow him. I glance at the living room on the right as we move to the room next to the office. The house, downstairs, is furnished with comfortable, traditional American furniture.

The first thing I see in the small bedroom is a wall of black-and-white framed photographs of major league baseball players. The dominant photograph is one of Jackie Robinson.

"I grew up in Boston, but I was a Brooklyn Dodger fan from the time I was a little kid," he says looking at Jackie Robinson. "They couldn't broadcast Sunday games in Boston because of the Blue Laws, but I could pick up the Dodgers on WHME. As a matter of fact, I'm in the process of signing a contract to do a novel about Jackie Robinson."

"You wrote a short story about him," I say.

"Right, for a collection of stories called *Murderers' Row*."

We move back into his office, he behind the desk, me in an armchair.

"Have you always lived in the Boston area?"

"Joan and I had a house in Los Angeles for a while. We used to go there for winters, but I just missed the Northeast, Boston, Baltimore, Philadelphia. Anyway, my father died in 1978 and my mother ten years later. My family now is Joan, me and the boys."

"You have two sons?"

"Yes, one is almost forty, an actor in Los Angeles, more a stage actor than movies and television, but he did play the priest, Father O'Hearn, in the A&E Spenser episode *Thin Air* and had a big role in a movie called *Don't Get Out of the Boat* a few years ago. Keep an eye out for it. My other son is forty-four, a choreographer in New York."

"And both of your sons are gay?"

"Yes and both are involved in the theater. Joan and I, particularly Joan, are gay rights advocates. She works for Community Servings which delivers meals to people with AIDS and with the Commonwealth Shakespeare Company and Theater Offensive, Boston's only gay theater."

"So you go to the theater a lot?"

"Not very much. I've seen a ton of stuff my sons have done, otherwise I rarely go. Now and then I'll go see a Shakespeare production, but generally Joan goes to the theater and then

reports back to me. I don't go out to movies either. I've seen about three movies in theaters in the last ten years."

"No television?"

"Baseball, Westerns, *Law & Order*. It's the best thing on television. One of the best things that's ever been on television. If I work it right, I can see four hours of *Law & Order* in a row on TNT and NBC."

"And what do you read?"

"Very little fiction. I just finished a biography of Harry Truman. I do reread Raymond Chandler and the Nero Wolfe novels. One of the charms about Rex Stout is that he wrote so many Wolfe novels, something like eighty, that by the time you get through reading them, you can start all over because you've forgotten them. Besides, I never understood how Wolfe solved the cases anyway. It's not a problem for me. It's the ride that counts. It's Archie, the house, the masculine world they live in."

I say, "I did a script for the Wolfe A&E series, *Immune to Murder*, the one where Wolfe and Archie go to the fishing lodge in upstate New York."

"I think the A&E Wolfe's are right on the money," Parker says. He turns his chair toward me.

"People think of you as a 'man's man.'"

"I'm a macho son-of-a-bitch," Bob says with a very small smile.

"Like Spenser," I say. "He's been shot more than nine times and always comes back with a sharp line and a wry smile."

Bob gives me a wry smile.

Kaminsky: Tell me about your family.
Parker: My parents? My biography? That sort of thing?

Yes.
My father was born in Belfast, Maine. He went to Colby College in Waterville, Maine and became an executive at Colby. My mother's parents were Irish immigrants. Her maiden name was Murphy. I graduated from Colby in 1954 with an English degree and joined the Army. I married Joan, who I'd met at Colby, in 1956. And then I went to grad school at Boston College, got an M.A. in 1957 and then went to work while I slowly earned my Ph.D. in English at Boston University.

Went to work?
Various jobs. One was working in public relations for Prudential Insurance. Then I got a job teaching English at Northeastern University. I got my Ph.D. in 1970. I became a college teacher, got tenure and a full professorship and stayed away from the faculty lounge. I didn't have to do anything so I didn't do anything except teach. I stayed away from the other teachers. University faculty members are amazing people. I'd been in the infantry in Korea and met some pretty bad people, but many, maybe most of the people I met in university life were the worst people I'd ever met. There is more backstabbing politics in a university department than in a national political election and as others have pointed out, it might be because there is less at stake in a university department. Now and then you do find a really good person in academia, but not often enough.

You taught English literature?
Mostly the classics.

That's why Spenser with an 's', in honor of the British classical poet?
Right. And my Spenser is also a published poet.

Which explains why the Spenser novels are filled with quotations from popular songs to lines from Shelley and Shakespeare. Was your doctoral dissertation about classical literature?
No, it was on the private eye, focused on Chandler, Hammett and Ross MacDonald. I don't remember the title but a 350 copy special edition of a cut down version with a lot of the academic stuff removed was published as *The Private Eye in Hammett and Chandler.*

So if you had to make a living other than writing, what would you do? Teach?
Hell no. I can do some carpentry. I don't do much of it anymore. Like anything else, you lose the skill. I have all the tools downstairs. I built one of the first houses Joan and I lived in. I suppose, elevated to my economic needs, I might want to be an architect. Next subject.

Okay, let's talk about Spenser on television. I liked the A&E movies with Joe Mantegna.
Good. I wrote the movies. And Joe is a very good actor who gave us a lot of creative leeway.

I didn't like Spenser for Hire. I watch it once in a while.
Yes, I didn't watch it very often either. By the time it went off the air, I was sick of it. I'd read every script and had been involved in development. I thought it was, you know, your standard private eye show. The A&E movies aimed much higher. I got last word on the scripts, other than A&E. Actors, directors couldn't change the script without my permission and I could veto any casting.

I know you like Joe Mantegna as Spenser, but have you ever thought of anyone else in the role?
Robert Mitchum would have been right.

You have an all-time favorite novel?
The Great Gatsby.

Let's talk about writing. What's your day like? Do you write every day?
Pretty much every day, five days a week. I do five pages a day. It's like running a small business. It's a job. I have letters to write and other stuff that has to be done. Later in the day I go to the gym and work out or take a walk. I come home and have supper, look at a ball game. That's pretty much what I do.

You're writing two other series. One about a small town police chief with drinking and relationship problems.
Jesse Stone. And the other series is about a female private eye, Sunny Randall. Sunny was literally inspired by Helen Hunt who was interested in bringing Sunny to the movies.

Religion. You're Irish Catholic.
I was raised Irish Catholic but I'm not anymore. I'm still Irish, but I'm no longer Catholic. I'm not unspiritual. I sort of think there must be more to all this. The mechanics and physics, all explanations of the universe are equally absurd. On the other hand I'm inclined to think that organized religion is the enemy of the Spirit. That doesn't deny the possibilities of something going on beyond our camp.

Is there anyone you particularly admire from history?
Harry Truman. Jackie Robinson, both for obvious reasons. Robinson was so great that it's incomprehensible.

Parker gets up to stretch and again motions for me to follow him. We keep talking as he shows me around the first floor of the house.

The downstairs of the house is his, and the second floor is Joan's. They each have privacy, but there is no doubt from what he says that he never wants to be further from his wife than downstairs.

"On the big issues," he says, "Joan and I are amazingly in tune but on the creature comfort level we're incompatible."

The marriage has been tested by a two-year separation and Joan's successful battle against breast cancer, which is chronicled in the 1978 book by Bob and Joan titled *Three Weeks in Spring*. More than thirty of Robert Parker's forty-one books are dedicated to his wife.

Joan, who retired as director of curriculum and instruction from the Massachusetts Department of Education, frequently writes with Bob, and they are co-owners of their own company, Pearl Productions.

We keep talking and when it is, by mutual unspoken agreement, time to end, we get up and Bob walks me to the front door.

"One last question," I say as we shake hands. "What about writer's block?"

"Writer's 'block'? That's just another word for 'lazy'."

LISA SCOTTOLINE

I edged forward on my pew in the gallery so I wouldn't miss a single word. My ex-lover's new girlfriend, Eve Eberlein, was about to be humiliated by the Honorable Edward J. Thompson. I wanted to dance with joy right there in the courtroom. Hell hath no fury like a lawyer scorned.

—*Legal Tender* by Lisa Scottoline

Lisa Scottoline, born Lisa Scottolini, has come a long way from the small city apartment where she raised her only daughter on her own and had difficulty paying the rent.

We sit in her huge, neatly trimmed yard—really a twenty acre field—behind her house in Bucks County, just outside of Philadelphia. There's a barn in the distance and a fenced area for horses.

"I'm just a city girl who can't believe I'm here. A great day for me is getting a good chapter done and coming to sit out here with a slice of pizza and a glass of Zinfandel and then maybe doing a little needlepoint. Other than that I like mowing, driving the tractor back and forth. I also grow basil and tomatoes. That's enough for me. My husband is the gardener."

Lisa went to the University of Pennsylvania law school, married, practiced law, and had a baby daughter. Soon after, she found herself divorced and broke with no alimony and no job, because she had decided to stay home and devote herself to raising her daughter KiKi, who is now eighteen.

"I wasn't really raised Catholic," she says. "My parents didn't go to church except for special occasions. I may be a closet atheist. Anyway, after my daughter was born, my mother wanted me to baptize her. I said no, that it would be hypocritical. I found out that when they were visiting me at least four of my cousins had taken my daughter into the kitchen, put water on her head and considered that the closest thing to a baptism that would save her soul. I wasn't angry for a change. It couldn't hurt and they could be right. It's insurance.

"I liked being at home," she says. "I didn't like being broke. I was working part time as a law clerk, definitely considered a step down for a lawyer. The bills piled up, credit cards were maxed. I started writing."

Quitting her job in a law firm, Lisa lived on credit cards for three years to write her first novel, *Everywhere that Mary Went*. HarperCollins bought it, paid her debts, picked up awards with her second book, *Final Appeal*, and three books later hit the *New York Times* bestseller list with *Mistaken Identity*.

"Until a few years ago, my credit was so bad that I couldn't get a credit card," she recalls. "When I finally did start to make money writing and had my bills paid, I could only get the lowest credit line on a card. I knew I finally had made a breakthrough when Neiman Marcus gave me a credit card."

Lisa is Italian on both sides of her family, and proud of it.

"You eat spaghetti for lunch every day?"

"Well, yesterday I had Slim Fast," said Lisa, petting a big yellow golden retriever named Lucy who is resting its head in her lap.

Other dogs, some of them Lucy's offspring, vie for our attention.

"They're Italian dogs," Lisa says. "They like to be around people."

A small bundle of energy, Lisa—neat, trim, petite and blonde—had just fed my wife and I a carb horror lunch of Philly Cheese Steaks and some fifty-cent delicacy called a Tasty Cake which consisted of two soft cookies with marshmallow filling between them. She wanted us to have genuine Philly food and then she remembered that she had forgotten to pick up canolis.

Lisa's father was an architect, quiet, hard working, from a family of farmers. Lisa's mother's family were, Lisa says, "Thieves. We always had the latest televisions and radios," she remembers. "My Uncle Mikey would drive up some afternoon with a truck full of bicycles and tell me to pick one. Christmas presents didn't come wrapped. They were just sitting there on the truck on Christmas morning."

Lisa had an Aunt Lena, her mother's sister, to whom no one in the family spoke to or about. Lisa discovered the reason was that they all thought Aunt Lena had brought a gun to Holy Communion.

"Everyone in my mother's family carried concealed weapons. My mother's family was from South Philly. Carrying your weapon to church was acceptable but, for some reason, not to Holy Communion. My father's family was West Philly, ten blocks away but considered to be much higher up on the social ladder, but it was more like the difference between a waiter and a bus boy. It was considered a mixed marriage."

Lisa's father went to the University of California in Berkeley on the GI bill and became an architect. Her mother worked as a secretary.

She has one brother, two years younger, who lives in the South Beach area of San Francisco.

She also has a half-sister she didn't know she had till about nine years ago when she answered a knock at her door.

"I opened the door," Lisa says, "and there stood someone who looked exactly like me, only with a beautiful body telling me she was both a fan and my half-sister. I was really pissed."

"Why?"

"I'm Italian. I wake up angry. I'm a lawyer. I love being a lawyer partly because I like to fight. Sound sick?"

I reply, "I lived in Rome for a while, that does sound very Italian."

"Almost anything can make me angry," she says. "Anger's okay. You're allowed to have anger if you've been raised the way I was. You're allowed to do everything at a high level, violently, including love, which is a good thing. My husband and I had a good fight last night. We were over it almost immediately. I don't carry grudges. My mother does. She has a series of superstitious beliefs, including one in which she believes what goes around comes around. She had one lifelong enemy. My mother would say, 'That woman will die for what she has done.' So, thirty years later the woman died and my mother said, 'See?' Superstition is my mother's religion."

"The woman at your door, the one who said she was your sister. You let her in and . . ."

"I immediately called my dad who, after a stunned silence, says, yeah, that he had an affair four years before I was born."

Lisa's sister, who was adopted, had been searching for her birth parents. She found her father, who had retained the family name, Scottolini, took a look at the photo on the back flap of one of Lisa's novels and put it together. Now the sisters are close friends. Lisa has dedicated a book to her.

Lisa uses a computer and is a hunt-and-peck typist who tries to finish twenty pages a day. She rewrites and rewrites, shoots for and gets one book finished per year. She doesn't work from outlines.

"When I started writing, I concentrated on screenplays," she says. "I wrote three of them. No responses from producers or agents. I would have been happy to get a rejection letter. Then I wrote my first novel and got an agent. This time I got rejection letters, lots of them, probably from every house that publishes in the English language."

By this time, Lisa had decided writing was fun. And being $38,000 in debt, she took the job as a law clerk and finished the novel. One month into the job, her novel was published as a paperback original. Shortly after that she was nominated for an Edgar Allan Poe Award. She moved onto hardcovers, remarried, and acquired two stepchildren, whom she loves.

Now it's time to talk about her work.

Kaminsky: What is your work schedule?
Scottoline: I like to work from nine A.M. to 2:30 P.M., but I'll work at night or early in the morning if I'm nearing a deadline. I write fifteen to twenty pages, a chapter or a complete section.

How do you know when a manuscript is going right?
When I feel like I'm having a conversation with the reader and I'm holding the reader's interest. I'm not just telling a story. I want you to love the story. I want you to love me. I want to entertain you. I'm not patient with a lot of contemporary fiction that sounds like the author doesn't care if I'm interested.

What's your favorite thing about being a writer?
I get to do it at home. I also like to tour with a new book. The fun part about touring is that you get to meet people who have read your books and love them. My favorite vacation spot is the Jersey shore.

Do you get the ideas for your books from your experience?
I get about an idea a year for a book and am always worried when I finish a book that I won't have an idea for the next one. I grab at ideas. There was my new-found half-sister coming through the doorway telling me this heartfelt story and I'm thinking, 'mistaken identity,' an idea, and I find a pad and a pen so I can write it down. The business with my mother and my Aunt Lena bringing the gun to Holy Communion was an idea that led to *The Vendetta Defense*.

You don't outline. Do you write a synopsis before you begin a book?
No, I just have the idea and I start writing.

Were your father or mother readers?
There were no books in our house. There was just the *TV Guide*. I was badly educated before I got to college.

Do you listen to music when you work?
No, music doesn't do it for me. I do like television. I have two television sets in my office so I can have two things on at the same time.

You are a very funny writer. Few legal thrillers have a sense of humor. In one of your books, you have all these jokes about Looney Tunes' characters. You have a character in dire stress, carrying stolen money, doped out on heroin with people trying to kill him and he can't stop thinking about how it's like being in a cartoon. Very funny.
What I try to do is keep things moving all the time, like moving Benny from problem to problem almost non-stop and then coming up with some way for her to get out of danger for the moment. I put her in a situation and she has to do something right now. I never plan. Like, shit, she's on top of the building. I have to get her down and she's surrounded by cops. My God, what am I going to do?

You get her down.
I'd better. My mortgage rides on it.

There are an almost infinite number of ways you can get her down, but you have to find one the reader will believe.
That's the hard part.

You blow that and you risk losing your reader.
I am haunted by my memory of being in a movie theater one night and hearing a boy behind me shout at the screen, "That couldn't happen."

Last questions. If you could have one super power, what would it be?
I'd want to be able to eat anything I wished and never gain weight. I'm a cake freak.

Politics?
I'm a liberal democrat.

If you could be one other person for a day, who would it be?
Madonna or any member of the Supreme Court.

Scalia? He's Italian.
He may be the one Italian in the world I don't like.

What are you going to do now?
I think I'll just ride my daughter's pony around in circles for a while. You never know. It might give me the idea I need for the next book.

JAMES LEE BURKE

*I removed the three roses I had placed in a vase two
nights previously and washed and refilled the vase under
a tap by the gravel path. That led through the cemetery.
Then I put three fresh roses in a vase and set it in front
of the marble marker that was cemented into the front
of Bootsie's crypt. The roses were yellow, the petals edged
with pink, the stems wrapped in green tissue paper by
a young clerk at the Winn-Dixie store in New Iberia.
When he handed me the roses I was struck by the bloom
of youth on his face, the clarity of purpose in his eyes. "I
bet these are for a special lady," he had said.*
—*Last Car to Elysian Fields* by James Lee Burke

James Lee Burke sits back in his chair and looks out the window of his kitchen through the light rain at the bayou about fifty feet away.

He is smiling. He smiles a lot.

He is looking at the flowing dark water and listening to the rain gently pelting his roof.

A familiar Western hat on his head, he sits back, and seems, at least for the moment, to be at peace in his home at the outskirts of New Iberia, Louisiana.

Jamie's wife Pearl is away visiting relatives. His children are grown and on their own. Their daughter Alafair bears the same name as the daughter of Dave Robicheaux, Burke's main character in *Last Car from Elysian Fields*. Jamie's daughter is a mystery novelist, a former deputy district attorney in Portland, Oregon, and a criminal law teacher at Hofstra Law School.

Jamie is spending a week doing what he is most comfortable doing, going to AA meetings, going to the Catholic church, spending time with his friends—mostly police officers and former officers—and writing.

The coffee is strong.

A white cat strolls over to Jamie who reaches down to touch its head as it passes.

"My family has lived here on the bayou, literally on the bayou, since 1836. I've been here all my life, in and out. My novel, *White Dove at Morning*, deals with my family, the Civil War, particularly the Battle of Shiloh and the Union occupation. That's my father's family, the Catholics. I deal with my mother's side, the Baptists, in *Cimarron Rose*. My great-grandfather Sam Holland appears in three of my books, as sort of a specter. He was a Confederate soldier and a gunfighter. I had part of his journal used in *Cimarron Rose*."

"Specter," I repeat. "There's almost always a touch of the mystical in your books. For example, the pelicans in *Last Car from Elysian Fields* that Bootsie may have sent to save Dave's life."

"I believe in spiritual presence," Jamie says. "To me it's a great mystery to believe that matter does not have a beginning or an end and requires no first cause and that the universe created itself and intelligence evolved out of non-intelligence without the intrusion of some other kind of agent. That requires a much greater leap of faith than a belief in the spirit. If we're the smartest things around, we're in deep trouble."

"So your religion is. . .?"

"Catholic," he says. "I'm a Catholic on my father's side. My mother's family were Baptists."

"So you are a practicing Catholic?"

"You bet. I go to church every week."

He glances over his shoulder out the window at the overcast sky. A barking dog trots by. A large gray swamp bird soars low about fifty feet away.

"There are miracles," he says with a smile and a sigh. "A bird flying through the sky is a miracle. I see miracles every time I open my eyes. For instance, everything in this house is a miracle. It all came from nothing. It came from a planet on which there was nothing, and we were given the power somehow to turn nothing into books, clocks, computers, rugs, cars. Miracles."

"When did you decide to become a writer?"

"My first cousin Andre Dubus and I grew up together, started writing when wc were young and remained close until he died in 1999 from injuries he received ten years earlier when he saved the lives of two motorists on I-93. Andre was a great short story writer. His son is also a wonderful writer."

The elder Dubus' short story "Killing" was the basis of the award-winning movie *In The Bedroom.*

Burke's career has seen its ups and downs. First published at age nineteen, by the time he was thirty-four he had four novels under his belt. But then, suddenly, publishers wanted nothing to do with him—yet, the novel they rejected for nine years, *The Get Lost Boogie*, would eventually earn a nomination for the Pulitzer Prize.

"You have any brothers or sisters?"

"I'm an only child," he says. "But Pearl and I have four children."

"You met Pearl in college."

"We met at the University of Missouri where she had come to get a master's degree in Library Science. We both got our degrees in 1960. Pearl was born in Beijing. Her family were refugees, got caught in the war between the Communists and Nationalists. When she was still a teenager, she got on a refugee boat for Formosa that was almost blown out of the water from mainland guns."

For years Jamie wrote unsuccessfully and worked at various jobs, including that of a forest ranger in Kentucky. With a recommendation from author Jim Hall, Jamie was offered a job teaching at the University of Montana.

Jamie goes to the window where a big dog is looking in, tongue out. It's the neighbor's dog, the one who had chased the bird a few minutes earlier.

"Sometimes he just stands patiently at the window and watches me work."

"You think there are particular authors who influenced you?"

He nods his head and answers with no hesitation, "Robert Penn Warren, Eudora Welty, Flannery O'Connor, Ernest Hemingway, James T. Farrell, Tennessee Williams and Gerard Manley Hopkins."

"Next question," I say. "The big one we all get asked. Where do you get your ideas? Or where does your inspiration come from?"

Jamie leans forward, folds his hands. It's a question he is quite willing to get into. "Shelley put it well. We murder to dissect. The Freudians maintain, and I think there's some truth to their theory, that neurosis provides a conduit to the unconscious. That's a clinical way of putting it. Shakespeare put it another way. He said all power comes from the world of dreams. Milton, in his sonnet on blindness, said he woke each day to darkness. His illumination was in his sleep."

"Religion, culture, do they play a role?"

"Possessing a historical culture through Judaism, or Christianity, or whatever background is important, as it allows humor. The fundamentalists are angry people because ultimately they have no confidence. Their behavior demonstrates the falsity of their belief. I'll never forget Golda Meir's great statement about the founding of Israel. She said the Hebrews are the only people in history who would wander for 2,000 years and find the only country in the Middle East that has no oil. Irish humor is like that, too. You hungry?"

It was a little after noon. Jamie called his friend C.J. LaBauve, a retired Louisiana state police officer. C.J. has a cop's bounce and knowledge of every street, shop and crime in their small town.

"What kind of food do you like?" I ask as we drive down a dirt road.

"If it doesn't fight back on the plate, I'm okay with it," says Jamie. "I like Cajun food, Mexican food."

"You speak Cajun?" I ask.

"Enough to get by," he says as we pull in front of a large shack with a hand-painted sign advertising shrimp. The shack looks like the one in *Sunset Limited*.

Inside everyone recognizes Jamie and C.J. as we sit down at a wooden picnic table and eat great plates of shrimp, catfish and gumbo from paper bowls.

"Some quick questions," I say over Styrofoam cups of Coca-Cola.

"Shoot."

Kaminsky: Writer's block?
Burke: Never had it. I think it's doodah. Hemingway said you can't just sit down and write one sentence. If you write one, you write two, and then three and you've got a paragraph. That's the way I do it some days.

You've taught creative writing classes. Can you teach anyone to write fiction?
You can help them with style, technique, suggest reading, but you can't give them talent.

What's your greatest achievement in writing? What are you most proud of?
The way my family has participated in my career and supported it all these years because we had so many lean years. We lived in old motels, in a garage. I filed for unemployment everywhere.

Do you have one favorite book of yours?
No, they're all my children and I love them for different reasons. I'd say the best writing I've done is *Purple Cane Road*, *Joelee Blount's Bounce*, *Black Cherry Blues*. *Cimarron Rose* and *Hart's War* are close behind.

Who do you see playing Robicheaux in a movie? I see Tommy Lee Jones.
Good actor. I've talked to Alec Baldwin. He's good, too. Harrison Ford has a natural quality about him. He comes across as an ordinary and decent American man who has far greater complexity inside him than people would guess. He emotes complexity.

You used to have a drinking problem.
Used to. I've been in a twelve-step program for more than twenty years. I'll be going to a meeting tomorrow night.

Your health?
Good.

We get back in the car again. It's still overcast, drizzling slightly. Jamie's friend, C.J. says he has something I might like to see. Jamie nods.

We cross a street, Burke Street.

"Your family?"

"That's right," Jamie says. "My great-grandmother ran a boarding house right there. She was a widow. Her son Willie Burke was in the Confederate army. And there."

He points to a house.

"My cousin lives right here. He's eighty-three years old. He was a prosecutor. His best known case involved a murder that took place right near my house."

We drive down the road just past Jamie's house and turn right onto a very narrow muddy road into a field. There's something familiar about it.

We stop the car in a spot next to a group of trees no more than twenty feet tall.

"*Dead Man Walking*," says C.J. as we get out of the car.

The feeling is uncanny. It looks to me exactly like the place where the girl is murdered in the movie, right down to the pickup truck tire tracks and the muddy ground.

"They were supposed to shoot the movie here," says Jamie. "But the city council decided not to cooperate because of the negative way my cousin was treated for the prosecution."

We get back in the car and Jamie suggests we end with something more positive about New Iberia. We drive to City Park, located just off of the two-block long main street of the town. The park is huge.

"There're picnic pavilions all over," says Jamie. "Swimming pool, recreation house. It never changes. There used to be an old green building. People still have crab boils, crawfish boils and barbecues in the evenings. C.J. and I saw Harry James play here. Andre and I used to sneak in the serving lines at anybody's picnic when we were kids."

On the way back to the bed and breakfast where my wife and I have been staying, we see more of the sights of New Iberia and pass through the two-block main street of the town. I notice a sign on one of the welcoming bayou shops and smile. It states, "Dave Robicheaux eats here."

TONY HILLERMAN

*I always wondered who invented the absurd lie that pro-
claimed there 'were no atheists in foxholes.' Where else could
atheism better thrive than in the killing fields where homicide
was honored? In the Third General Hospital at Aix, the poker
game was about as religious as things got.*
—*Seldom Disappointed, a Memoir* by Tony Hillerman

My most vivid memory of Tony Hillerman is the night I presented him with the Mystery Writers of America's highest honor, the Grandmaster award for lifetime achievement.

When I gave my introduction, Tony strode calmly to the podium in front of a thousand people, took out his notes and gave a short sincere speech to great applause. Then he went back to his table at the back of the ballroom. I reached for my notes only to find that Tony, who had appeared so calm in his acceptance, had nervously picked them up and walked off with them.

Tony is seventy-eight years old. His wife of over fifty years, Marie, is out shopping when he opens the door of their modest adobe home just outside of Albuquerque a few hundred yards from the Rio Grande River.

Marie once told me that her husband's absent-mindedness had nothing to do with aging.

"One time, years ago," Marie, a petite slim woman with a knowing smile, told me, "Tony had to give an award to Mary Higgins Clark who we've known for years and years. When it came

time to say, "and I give you Mary Higgins Clark," Tony forgot her name. Mary, knowing Tony, hurried up and with a smile gave her name. Tony's even forgotten my name when he has had to introduce me to other people."

I asked Tony about his infamous memory.

"I've never been any good with names. I got you screwed up with an agent the last time I talked to you on the phone. I even introduced my wife as Mildred shortly after we were married. Once, at a reception at a Navajo Tribal Fair, I went over to join Marie who was talking to this nice looking man. She introduced me to him and he kept asking me questions about my books. I was getting a little embarrassed and decided to change the subject, so I asked what line of work he was in. 'I'm the Governor of New Mexico,' he said."

While he may have trouble with names, Tony Hillerman has an almost uncanny ability to remember the minute details of a World War II battle he was in over a half a century ago.

I had recently read Tony's memoir *Seldom Disappointed.*

Tony was born in Sacred Heart, Oklahoma, the youngest of three children. His mother was Lucy Grove and his father, Augustus, was a farmer and storekeeper.

Tony went to St. Mary's Academy, a boarding school for Indian girls near a Benedictine mission for the Citizen Band Potawatomi Tribe in Sacred Heart from 1930 to 1938. Besides him there were only a handful of boys in the school. He took a bus to Konawa High School and graduated in 1942 when he went to work on the family farm.

A short time later, Tony's father died and Tony at the age of seventeen joined the U.S. Army. He served in combat on a mortar team and was awarded the Silver Star, the Bronze Star with Oak Leaf Cluster and the Purple Heart. In one vivid exchange, the boy found himself face-to-face with a German soldier holding an automatic weapon. Tony got off the first shot and killed the soldier.

In 1945, he stepped on a land mine suffering two badly broken legs, a foot and an ankle, painful facial burns, and temporary blindness. He came very close to death in a military hospital.

After the war he attended the University of Oklahoma and earned a bachelor's degree in 1948. He found work as a reporter in Oklahoma and New Mexico and then with United Press. He earned a graduate degree in English from the University of New Mexico in 1966 and joined the faculty. From 1976 to his retirement in 1981 he served as chairman of the Department of Journalism.

"One third of your memoir is devoted to the two years of your life during World War II," I say as we sit in his neat, sunny office in the front of his house.

Tony leans back, hands behind his head.

"The War," he says. "I'm one of those guys that never got over the war. I mean nobody had invented post-traumatic syndrome and all that crap yet. After the war, I spent a year or so throwing up after I ate breakfast."

Tony leans back and touches a pen on his desk.

"You were raised Roman Catholic."

"Still am," he says. "When my arthritis is bothering me, I go for a walk and look up. I just pray, thank the Lord for caring enough about us to give us all this beauty."

Through the window we can see a mountain range that seems movie perfect.

"Have you ever gotten in trouble because of something you wrote in one of your books?"

"Yes," he says. "One of my books, *Skin Walkers,* was banned in Colorado Springs, a center of the religious right, because it had witchcraft in it. I got a call from someone in Colorado who wanted me to publicly display my outrage. I said, to tell the truth, I'm impressed when moms and dads care enough about what their kids read to complain about it."

"You were a reporter for years, covered politics. What are your politics?"

"I'm a John L. Lewis Democrat which means I'm totally obsolete. I'm a blue-collar working class Democrat. The Democratic Party has been gobbled up by the power structure, by the

social elite. I voted for Kennedy, covered the convention when he was nominated, and I'm proud to say Pierre Salinger called me a son-of-a-bitch and Lyndon Johnson called me a dirty son-of-a-bitch."

"You and Marie have a large family, all adopted except for Ann. What made you and Marie want to do this?"

"We had Ann first," he says. "And she was fun. We found out we couldn't have more children for medical reasons. I grew up with a brother and sister and Marie grew up with a brother, sister and adopted sister. I like children. Marie loves them. We wound up with five adopted children."

"How often do you get together with the whole family?"

"Just before you arrived I took some of the kids to the airport. They're scattered all over the place. Tony, my oldest boy, lives in Texas. He has two horses. We go down there about once a year for a family rally."

The doorbell rings.

"Marie's back. She's just letting me know."

"What's your work day like?"

"I usually get up about 7:30 in the morning. Marie's been up an hour or two by then. I have a cup of coffee and some toast, which usually takes me about an hour. Then I clean off my desk. It's uncharacteristically clean now. Then I write, usually in spurts. Actually, a lot of my writing is done when I'm trying to go to sleep at night or driving somewhere or picking up something from a casual conversation. If we weren't talking right now, I'd be working on the first chapter of my next book."

Marie walks in and says hello. Tony asks her if she would make us some coffee.

"Ordering me around again," she says with a smile and then ducks back out the door.

"How did you get interested in Indian culture?"

"Way back, Norman Cousins at the *Saturday Review* asked me to do an article on the pecking order of the Indian Tribes. I was hooked. People tend to think of the Indians as an homogenized group, but I found that the Navajo are as different from Zunis or Hopis as the Mormons are from the Buddhists. The Navajo are latecomers, possibly from Mongolia. God knows where the Zunis came from, probably from Asia, maybe out of South America."

"We're using the word 'Indian'," I say. "Not politically correct?"

"Indians want to be called Indians," Tony says emphatically. "Except for politically correct wannabe Indians. They want to be called indigenous people. The Indians, the Navajo, no matter what we do to them, they endure."

"Like Dilsey in Faulkner's *The Sound and the Fury?*"

"Yes. I love that book and since we've digressed, I think Faulkner's "The Bear" is the best short story every written."

"There's a story that Robert Redford called you and wanted to meet that night about doing a Leaphorn/Chee movie, but you said you couldn't."

"I had a poker game. The older players understood. The younger ones thought it was incredible. They couldn't believe I'd let a card game take precedence over a meeting with Robert Redford."

"Redford didn't think this was the least bit incredible?"

"No, he understood it was just something I had to do."

"But the movie was made."

"Yes, it was called Dark Passage with Lou Diamond Phillips as Chee and Fred Ward as Leaphorn. When they finished shooting and editing, Redford called and asked if I wanted to take a look at a rough-cut. He said it was all finished but the soundtrack. He wanted to know if I wanted to take my name off the picture. That's a pretty good tip-off. I've never seen it."

"I have. It's not bad. I think Fred Ward's particularly good as Leaphorn. Let's get back to the novels. You age Leaphorn and Chee."

"A little bit, but we're talking about a time span of thirty years. Leaphorn is retired, but if I had them both age, Chee would be retirement age now, in his late sixties and Leaphorn would be over ninety. I need Chee as a young man, sexually attractive to young woman. It's fiction. All my characters seem real to me and Chee always seems young to me and Leaphorn is in his late sixties."

"Since Leaphorn retired, do you find it difficult to bring him back into the novels?"

"Not very much," says Tony. "I've established him as a legendary figure. Everybody knows him and he lives right there in Window Rock."

"Why did you decide to call him Leaphorn? It's not a real Indian name is it?"

"No, in the first book he was going to be a minor character, just a cop an anthropologist goes to for some information. I asked myself 'What's a good name for an Indian cop?' I had just finished reading Mary Renault's *The King Must Die* and I was in the chapter where she's describing these guys jumping over the horns of a bull, Leaphorn."

"You've had a number of professions: journalist, teacher, author. Is there any other profession you would have enjoyed?"

"Historian or archaeologist. I think I'd rather be an historian than an archaeologist. If I were young and full of energy, this would be a good time to be a sociologist."

Marie comes in with coffee. We thank her and each take a cup. She moves out of the room as Tony picks up his cup and watches her leave.

Time has gotten away from us, and I have an afternoon plane to catch. We finish our coffee and Tony walks me into the kitchen where we put down our cups. Marie moves back into the living room with us. There are a number of crucifixes on the walls and shelves, not a lot, all small, mostly wood and modest.

"Do you read Tony's manuscripts?"

"No," she says touching his arm. "But he'll read passages to me, ask, 'What do you think of this, Marie?'"

"You have any regrets? Things you haven't done or written?"

He pauses a moment, purses his lips and says, "I started a novel, *The Death of the Party*, I'd like to finish about a real case. Just before we moved to New Mexico, there was a murder or an accident. A girl named Cricket Cooper jumped or was pushed out of a car to get away from Joseph Montoya, who later became a U.S. Senator. He was about to be Lieutenant Governor. The people involved picked her up and buried her in a ditch. Some rabbit hunters found her. They saw a hand sticking up out of the sand. Before it was all over a sheriff and an assistant

district attorney were in federal penitentiary and martial law was declared in the county where the girl died. It destroyed the Democratic Party in New Mexico and the Republicans took over. A mess, but a very interesting mess. I can't get it out of my mind."

At the open door, I'm about to step into the twenty-four degree early evening. Tony looks out at the mountains, lost in the memory of a dead girl he had never known.

"Maybe I'll get back to it," he says.

ANN RULE

*Fear often begins with the slightest niggle that something
taken for granted can no longer be trusted. A slice of a
shadow darkens a spot that only a moment before was
sunny, and a chill draft destroys what was warm and cozy.*
—*And Never Let Her Go* by Ann Rule

The ballroom of the Hyatt Hotel in Sarasota is packed with people, 550 people on folding chairs, looking up at a short, plump woman with a gentle smile. She could be your favorite aunt or the schoolteacher you felt comfortable confiding in at grade school.

But these people are waiting for Ann Rule to tell them the story of a grisly, heart-wrenching murder that took place in Sarasota, Florida, the town where I live. Ann wrote *With Every Breath You Take* about the brutal murder of Sheila Bellush who was killed in front of her triplet toddlers.

Ann wrote the book because Sheila's sister had contacted Ann saying that Sheila wanted her to write the story of her murder should her former husband ever find her and have her killed.

Before Ann speaks, the audience listens to various police and forensic experts who worked on the case tell about their participation in the investigation.

When Ann begins, the audience is silenced by her moving compassion for the victim and her family—a compassion that makes the murdered woman come to life.

Since she began writing about true crimes with *The Stranger Beside Me*—the story about Ted Bundy—whom, in an eerie coincidence, she knew personally—Ann has become a remarkably prolific and incisive chronicler of fascinating books of men who prey on and kill women. What strikes at the heart of the reader and what makes Ann a master of her genre, is her empathy with and sympathy for the victims, the friends and family of the victim and the law enforcement officials who put their souls into their work.

She tells about compulsions and motives of the killers, but it is the victims she honors by refusing to let them become detached portraits or crime scene mannequins.

On the morning after her talk, Ann comes to our house for breakfast. Ann is a cat person. We have three cats who are instantly comfortable with her. Over coffee after breakfast, we sit by our bay window on a cool, bright spring day.

I begin by saying, "One of the people in the audience last night asked if you've ever heard from any of the killers you've written about, and you said that you had."

"Yes," Ann says petting one of the cats. "I wrote a book called *Fever in the Heart*."

"I've read it," I say. "That's the one about the wrestling coach who got a student to kill another coach because the wrestling coach was in love with the victim's wife."

"Yes, the young man, Chuckie, was bound for the Olympics, but went to prison instead.

Anyway, when he got out, he left a message on my machine that we should meet because I should have had the guts to write about his side of the story. He left his phone number on my machine. I decided that if he meant to hurt me or kill me he wouldn't leave his phone number. I returned his call and talked to his wife. He never called again."

"Was anyone in your family a writer? Your parents?"

"No. My parents were both teachers. My father, Chester R. Stackhouse, was a pretty famous football, track and basketball coach. My mother taught developmentally challenged students. Because of my father's career, we moved frequently hitting such towns as Saginaw, Michigan, Salem, Oregon and Slippery Rock, Pennsylvania. He was track coach at the University of Michigan when Fritz Chrysler was there and Tom Harmon was on the football team. My father also coached at Lincoln University, a black university in Pennsylvania. And then we went to various schools, including Stanford, where he got his master's degree and coached the track team. His star athlete was the Olympic decathlon gold medalist Bob Mathias."

"How far back can you go in your family history?"

"Well," she says as the cat strolls away, "my maternal great-great-grandparents came over from Germany. Their name was Koth. My great-grandmother's name was Carolyn Weistinger. That's as far back as I know on that side. My grandpa Christian Hanson was a sheriff. His father had been an important politician in Copenhagen, Denmark. I've never been able to find real evidence, but I think he was a socialist. My uncle's name was actually Karl Marx Hanson. On my dad's side, I know my great- great-grandfather fought in the Civil War. His name was Malanthon Farnsworth. He was in the Ohio militia."

"Where did you go to grade school?"

"Bond School, Saginaw, Michigan, and then Bath School in Ann Arbor. I went to Flauson Junior High School and one year at Ann Arbor High School. Then I graduated from Coatesville High in Coatesville, Pennsylvania."

"What kind of kid were you?"

She smiles and shakes her head.

"Actually a pretty nice kid. I was a reader. I'd curl up at the apple tree with a book and stay there all day on a limb reading. I remember spending my summers in jail in Stanton, Michigan where my grandmother used to feed the prisoners. I remember one sweet woman in an upstairs cell who taught me how to crochet. She was about to go on trial for murder. I guess that was the beginning of my curiosity about criminal behavior."

"Your most vivid memories as a child?"

"Snow. We lived in Ann Arbor when I was ten, right next to a golf course. The winters were tough. I remember walking home from school across that golf course in whiteouts, frightened because I wasn't sure what direction I was going. I remember one winter when we lived in Cadillac the snow drifts were eighteen feet deep."

"You have any brothers or sisters?"

"I had a brother, Don, who committed suicide when he was twenty-one. He was about to graduate from college, an A student and had been accepted at Yale Medical School, but he suffered from clinical depression. That was in 1954, before the rise of anti-depressants."

"Is there a history of depression in your family?"

"Nope. I have a close extended family. My mother had four sisters and a brother. They all had kids. I have lots of cousins. I have five children, three grandchildren. My daughter Leslie is also a writer. She wrote *Whispers from the Grave*, *Kill Me Again* and *Coast to Coast Ghosts—True Stories of Hauntings across America*. My daughter Laura works with children of battered women and the elderly. My son Andy works in consumer research and drives a cab. Loves it. My son Mike manages my office. He has a degree in business administration from Washington State University. And don't forget Bruce, my foster son, Bruce Sherles. Bruce works in the cookie industry. Bruce is black. He moved in when he was thirteen. He's thirty-two now. Drives a truck, has two little kids."

"You kept the name Rule."

"Yes," she says. "The marriage didn't work out, but I like the name. Actually, we were in the process of getting divorced when my husband was diagnosed with melanoma. He was a fair-skinned, freckled blue-eyed blonde who had been a lifeguard all his life. He once swam Lake Washington, twenty-eight miles, the second person in history to do it. He died at forty-three from the melanoma."

"You must have had very big houses with all those children."

"Very big, but about ten years ago I moved to a small one bedroom house on Puget Sound."

"What did you do with the big house?"

"My son, Mike, bought it from me."

I pour more coffee and Ann asks if she can check her e-mail on my computer. We go up the stairs to my office and she goes online. There are hundreds of messages. She scans them quickly to see if there are any really urgent ones.

"I try to answer them all," she explains squinting at the screen.

My office, where we sit, is small, an 1890's teacher's desk, complete with inkwell, an equally old two-drawer table, handmade heavy wooden bookshelves and piles of books and clutter.

"Nothing looks urgent," she says, clicks off the computer and looks at one of the bookshelves.

"What do you read?" I ask sitting in an old cushioned rocking chair that badly needs regluing.

"My favorite author is Anne Tyler," she said. "I know it sounds funny because I write such horror stories of human behavior. I need time to read the other side. I prefer non-fiction to fiction. Given my choice, I'll read a medical book. I'm particular about writers getting the forensics right. I know it's impossible to get everything right."

I mention that one of the people in the audience the night before had said that Ann wrote about a certain flower blooming on the street in Sarasota where Sheila Bellush lived. The audience member said there was no such flower on that street.

"The audience member," Ann said, "was right." The flower had been misidentified by a police officer who had driven her around the neighborhood. "You can't get it all right," she says. "But I try. I try to verify my facts from at least three different sources."

"Do you have a personal formula for writing?"

"Yes," she said folding her hands. "I want to start the book at a place in the story where if a reader is in a bookstore and picks it up, the first page will grab him. The reader will want to know what happened. Then I set the stage, let them know something shocking has happened but not what it is. I'll then go back to the beginning, trace the lives of the principal players, the victim, the killer, the family, the investigators, even go into their family histories. Once I've set all that up, I follow the story in a linear fashion until I come to the point where I opened the book and then I tell the rest of the story. It's just something I've devised. It seems to work. I try to set place, let the reader know what it looks like, even what grows there and what the weather is, what they eat."

"You've written nineteen books and more than 1400 articles. How much of this has been fiction?"

Her answer is immediate. "One book. *Possessions*. It was based on a true case in New York. I moved it to Washington State. I made up my characters and theme. I set up the scenes and the characters did things I didn't expect. It was like they were alive."

"If it's working, that's what I think is supposed to happen."

"I would get up in the morning," she says, "just to see what they were going to do. I hope I can do more fiction. In my novel I created a mythical town, a combination of three counties in Washington. People still tell me they've looked for the town and can't find it."

"Do you have any idea for a novel you'd like to do?" I ask.

"I'd like to do a sequel to the novel I did, but my publisher says, 'We'll talk about this later, Ann.'"

"What are your politics?"

"I'm a Democrat, basically, although I vote for the candidate. If there's a Republican candidate I like a lot better than the Democratic candidate, I'll vote for the Republican. On most issues I'm liberal. I couldn't do it myself, but I basically believe a woman has a right to choose abortion. On racial issues I'm extremely liberal, because my dad taught us from the time we were little kids not to be prejudiced against anybody."

"What about capital punishment?" I ask. "You've written about some killers you've called 'monsters.'"

"Let's step back a little," she says. "I've been a true crime writer for thirty years. Among other things, before I began to write, I was a caseworker for the Washington State Department of Public Assistance. I was a social worker. I used to think that most people who were mean and did terrible things were unhappy, but then I discovered sociopaths, people who will always kill given a chance. I found out that the caseworker at the desk next to mine was Ted Bundy. To put it simply, I'm for the death penalty. I think of the victims yet to be out there who never hurt anybody. They're the ones who should get the benefit of the doubt."

"No life in prison without parole for these sociopathic killers?"

"No, because things change, new governors come in. There are always new criminals for the lay public to be intrigued with and people forget what some of those lifers have done. Some of the people I've written about are being locked up for twenty or thirty years. They tend to make ideal prisoners as did the first two killers I wrote about who went back to kill when they were released after twelve years. If we could guarantee, really guarantee, that they couldn't get out, I'd be willing to keep them in."

"Then these people are. . .?"

"Addicted to murder. That's my diagnosis. Murder for them is like any other substitute—drugs, alcohol, gambling. They can control it for a while, but it comes back and takes control."

"Ted Bundy?"

The Stranger Beside Me was Ann's book about serial killer Ted Bundy. She described him as a kind, considerate man who always walked her to her car at night after work.

"Bundy got out of control. He had to kill more and more to feel normal."

"He had to kill to feel normal?"

"Yes."

"What part does religion play in your life given the kind of people you write about?"

"I'm Protestant. I was baptized Lutheran, but not till I was grown up because my dad went to the Church of Christ in Ohio, which believes you should be grown up enough to make your own choice about being baptized. When my kids were born, I wanted them to be baptized, and at that point I was going to a Lutheran Church. So two are Lutheran, and the others are Methodists. I'm not a good churchgoer but I'm a lot stronger believer in my sixties than I was when I was twenty-five."

"Considering the monsters you've encountered, the innocent victims . . ."

"You wonder how I can still believe? Well, I believe in God. I believe in Jesus. I believe in Heaven. I believe you can turn your life over to Christ in a single moment and be forgiven. I actually had a moment like that, and I'm not ashamed of it. I'd gone to Hollywood in

1978. I had to make a decision about leaving my kids with babysitters. I had been making between $14,000 and $15,000 a year writing primarily for *True Detective* and *True Confessions*. A producer wanted me to write a screenplay based on an article I had written for *Cosmopolitan*. They had me sign a contract that said they owned the rights forever and the novel I would write based on the crime. So, instead of writing a novel based on the article, I wrote a true crime book. I went to Hollywood with the idea of staying six weeks. I stayed six months working in a five-by-ten room with no air conditioning, typing so that my neck and back hurt. They finally let me go and I found out they had hired another writer. I got $7,500 for six months of ten-hour days. I spent my weekends alone. I was lonesome, missed my kids and there I was without work. I actually got down on my knees and said, 'God, I thought I could handle this and be in charge, but I'm not doing well. I'm going to give the power back to you.' And things changed. I began to do what I felt I had to do, help victims."

"So you had a choice, but the addicted sociopaths don't?"

"I think people have free will, think they can choose evil, can choose good. I'm not sure we'll come around again. If you're a serial killer. . ."

"This sounds like reincarnation."

"I know. I have repetitive dreams of being another person in another time. I never thought I was Cleopatra. I've dreamed of being a child in London and working in a factory, being so tired, never seeing grass or trees. I have one dream in which I'm a rich woman who jumps into a stream when a child is drowning."

"Okay, I'll ask you a tough one. Do you believe somebody has to believe in Christ to go to Heaven?"

"No. There are good people in this world who never know about Christ. If you're Jewish, you don't believe in Christ as the Messiah."

"An earthbound question. Do you exercise?"

"I walk. I got a new hip on my right side about a year ago, but I walk."

"How do you choose which book you are going to do next?"

"I look for a protagonist, an anti-hero who has all those things that most people want, someone physically attractive, healthy, charismatic, popular, talented. Then when they murder once, twice or more and are arrested, people are shocked. Those are people who never get enough. They're empty inside and don't care who dies as long as they are happy or think they are."

"So something just clicks and you say, 'This is the next one'?"

"Yes, but at any given time there might be twelve out there. Some of it is a matter of timing. I like to go to the whole trial. So, if I'm working on a book or on tour, I can't do that story. Also, the crime has to be within the last three years unless, as with the Green River case I'm working on now, something new comes up. I've got a great case that happened in 1972 but it's too old. I might go back and do a classic from a hundred years ago, and I'm not going to fight other writers by doing high profile cases like O.J. or Jean Benet Ramsey.

"Any other conditions?"

"Yes, if the killer has served his or her time and they are out, I won't write the book. I don't want to make it hard for them to start over."

"Your work schedule?"

"I work seven days a week and demand ten pages a day. I'm a slow starter. I get up, read the newspaper, eat breakfast, and answer e-mail for a couple of hours. I probably start writing about 10:30 and go till 7:30 or eight P.M."

"Do you ever do more than ten pages?"

"Oh yes. If I'm on a roll, I can do thirty, but that's usually because I'm doing verbatim testimony. Some days ten pages feel like forty-two, but if they're bad I can always go back and fix them. When I'm done my manuscripts are usually between 800 and 900 pages."

"Talk about research."

"Research, which includes the trial and interviewing," she says. "And the research goes on while I work on the book. People write to me with more information. Thank God for computers. I can simply paste the good material in. If the research is going well, I have to remind myself to get up and walk around so the blood doesn't settle in my ankles. The hours just pass. I have a little cabin next to my house so I can go to work in my pajamas. I just walk over. I used to write in my second bedroom, but with all of the files I work with, it was spreading into my house."

"What worries you about your writing?"

"What happens if the office burns down during the night? I used to put my disks in the refrigerator. Then if the house burns down, it probably won't burn my refrigerator. When I reach that stage, I know I'm happy with the book so far. When I had a mudslide in 1997, it was horrendous, catastrophic. It cost half a million dollars to fix. When it hit, I was working on two books. I got two of those big green garbage bags and threw the research and photos for one book in one bag and the material for the second book in the other. You always wonder what you'd save in a disaster. I saved my books. I knew the cats got away and I brought the dogs with me, but the most important thing was to save the books. I make as many as six back-up disk copies of every book and stash them. I send one home with my best friend. One's in a safe. One's at my son's house. One is stashed in my bra."

"You're favorite part about doing a book?"

"The trials. It's almost like a vacation. I go to another city, get a hotel room with a kitchen. I like the writing, too. What I don't like is the touring although once I get wherever I'm going, I love meeting people who read and like my books because writing is so lonesome. It's good to know there are people out there reading your books. It's especially fun to actually see one of them reading. Obviously, I don't like the running to airports, the heavy bags, being searched."

"How many dogs do you have?"

"Two. All my dogs have been mongrels. Holly was seventeen, painful arthritis, when she died a few years ago. I had to put her down. I got a puppy to replace her. The other dog is Lucy."

"How many cats?"

"Baby, Beanie, Bunny and Toonsit."

"You've got cutsie names for your animals?"

Ann, with a laugh, answers, "I'm not going to name them after serial killers."

"Any fan questions bother you?"

"Not a question really. When a person comes up to me and says, 'I'm waiting for the right time to write. I'm going to have a cabin in the woods where the muse will come and sit on my shoulder.' Well the muse is a lot of kids looking at you who you know are going to be hungry so you put your bottom in the chair and sit at the typewriter and do something. I always tell people, 'I don't want to know what your problems are. If you can't do it now, you're never going to do it.'"

"People frequently ask me which of my books is my favorite," I say. "I used to tell them, 'The last one' or 'I like them all.' But recently I've begun to single out some books. Do you have one that is especially important to you?"

"*The Stranger Beside Me* was special because it was my first and because I knew Ted Bundy personally. *Small Sacrifices* was particularly important because it was my breakout book, my first real bestseller. I also like *Death by Sunset*, *Never Let Her Go* and *Every Breathe You Take*. Oh, and *Everything She Ever Wanted*. I guess I like most of them."

"What makes you angry?"

"Injustice. I'm very, very slow to anger, but I can almost count on the fingers of one hand the times I've been angry over the last ten years. I get angry when people are mean to someone who can't fight back. I admit I get angry when people criticize my work unjustly. If they find mistakes and mention them, it's okay, but if I see a review and it isn't true, I get angry."

"Is there anyone in history you particularly admire?"

"Abraham Lincoln. He seemed like such a melancholy, brave good man and, of course, he was murdered."

"Any contemporaries you admire?"

"I don't get asked that question but I do have an answer: Oprah. I've been on her show four times. She came from such desperate circumstances and yet she has overcome the odds and is a genuinely nice person. She's always been nice to me whether the cameras are on or off."

"Regrets?"

"I wish I had started writing books sooner. I also wish I'd lost weight last week but I never seem to. My marriage wasn't good, but I don't regret it. Without it I wouldn't have the kids."

"Have you ever collaborated with anyone?"

"Yes. Twice. In my early writing days there was a sewer commissioner in Lake Washington. He wanted his autobiography written. I got a hundred dollars a chapter. There were ten chapters. He had three goals in life: to be sewer commissioner, to climb Mount Fujiama, and to write his autobiography. I guess that was collaboration. I also worked with a director named Martin Davidson on a screenplay that never got made. People are always writing me saying they want me to write the story of their life. We'll split 50/50 or worse, they offer me ten percent."

"We all get that. How do you deal with it?"

"I just tell them I don't collaborate. And that's the truth."

"Who are your friends?"

"My friends tend to be other writers like Donna Quinn, Donna Anders, Ann Combs, Jenny Okomoto, Margaret Chittenden. We have a group in Seattle called "The Bitch and Moan Society." We used to get together once a month but tours are getting in our way. I have a lot of friends who are policemen, detectives, lawyers, and prosecutors, people I've met through my writing. I have another group. We call ourselves "The Wild Women." We get together a couple of times a year. Columnists, prosecutors, detectives and writers, eight or ten of us and we swear that nothing we say when we get together will leave the room. Everyone knows secret stuff."

Kaminsky: Here come the quick questions. Try to answer without stopping to think. Writers block.
Ann: Can't afford it.

The source of creativity is . . .
Inborn. A gift from God.

Other talents besides writing?
I'm a pretty good artist. I draw, paint with oils.

What would you like to be if you weren't a writer?
A cop.

Favorite singers?
Frank Sinatra, Rosemary Clooney, Sarah Vaughn, Harry Connick, Jr.

What's a great day for you?
An October day in Michigan or Washington State when the leaves are changing.

Where do you like to shop for clothes?
Resale shops for clothes and for things I collect like miniature bottles, antique bottles.

What do you think you got out of your formal education?
Awareness of the arts, the ability to look for new experiences. Meeting deadlines.

It's getting dark. We go downstairs where my wife and daughter are and then we drive a tired Ann Rule around Sarasota showing her the white sand beaches and the Gulf of Mexico. When we drop Ann at her hotel, I have one more question.

"Do you stay in touch with the people you write about?"

"Most of them. Because it's not like I make friends with them because I just want information and then want to move on. I'm in touch with almost everybody from earlier books and readers who want to know what those people are doing now. With the persmission of the people I've written about, I give a general update on their well being on my website."

Ann says goodbye.

A beautiful white heron lands gracefully on the sidewalk in front of the hotel door. Ann walks gently around it and looks back at it with a smile.

[Ann Rule photographed at her home.]

MICKEY SPILLANE

He was only a little judge. He was little and he was old with eyes like two berries on a bush. His hair was pure white and wavy and his skin was loose and wrinkled. But he had a voice like the avenging angel. The dignity and knowledge behind his face gave him the stature of a giant, the poise of Gabriel reading your sins aloud from the Great Book and condemning you to your fate.
—*One Lonely Night* by Mickey Spillane

Mickey Spillane lives not in the New York City of his novels, but in the small coastal peninsula town of Murrells Inlet, South Carolina. He has lived there for forty-eight of his eighty-five years.

Mickey is compact, hair cut almost as short as he wore it when he was a fighter pilot in World War II. A small stroke several years ago hasn't slowed him down. When he walks, he bounces, and when he sits and talks he uses his hands and body and looks you straight in the eye. He is a man of tremendous enthusiasm with a passion for ice-skating, which he does twice a week at an indoor rink in Charleston.

Mickey's father, John, a bartender in Brooklyn, and a heavy smoker, died of lung cancer at the age of seventy. John was the one who gave him the nickname Mickey. His mother, Anne, called

him Babe. Anne was a Scotch Protestant. John was an Irish Catholic.

Mickey spends much of his time in a small comfortable library at the front of his three-story wooden house. On the shelf behind him is a small bust of Edgar Allan Poe given to Mickey when he was named a Grandmaster by the Mystery Writers of America. Next to it is an odd plaque. The plaque reads, "This is your Oscar. Thanks to Mickey Spillane for three billion cases of beer sold. Lite All-Star Banquet, February 12, 1991. Bel Air Hotel." Mickey was a spokesperson for Miller for nineteen years.

Next to the plaque is an old framed newspaper photograph. The very young Frank Morrison who would become Mickey Spillane is in a small boat with the name *Wonder Boy* written in black on the side. The caption reads: *Captain of the Lifeguards Mickey Spillane demonstrates the actual technique used in lifesaving and water safety as prescribed by the American Red Cross.*

Before the war, Mickey had made a living writing comic books for Funnies, Inc., which later became Marvel Comics, and short stories for pulp magazines.

He wrote Nick Carter books, lots of series, under lots of different names. "Once I was reading a book in the New York Public Library in Manhattan," he recalls, "and I thought, wow, what an ending. I checked it out and found out I'd written the book."

Then the war came.

At the end of the war, Mickey was stationed in Greenwood, Mississippi where he met and married Mary Ann Pearce. Mickey was a captain at the time of his discharge. When he got out of the army, he played football at Kansas State Teachers College in Fort Hayes, Kansas. Mary and Mickey had four children: Kathleen, Ward, Michael and Caroline.

Mickey went back to doing Fawcett comic books: *Captain America*, *Captain Marvel*, *The Human Torch*, *Submariner*. Then he did a comic called *Mike Danger*. *Mike Danger* became *I, The Jury* with the paperback market in mind. After four publishers rejected it saying there

was no market for paperback originals, he brought it to Roscoe Fawcett at Gold Medal Books. Fawcett liked it and took it to New American Library. New American took it to Dutton and said they would immediately reprint it in paperback if Dutton published some copies in hardcover. The year was 1947. Mickey got a $1,000 advance and made history.

New American Library printed 7,000 hardcovers and put it out at Christmas. They followed with the printing of a quarter of a million. It sold out in two days. It's still selling today. Now, fifty-six years later, more than 130 million copies of Mickey Spillane books have been sold. Thirteen of those books feature Mike Hammer.

Ayn Rand, who wrote *The Fountainhead* and *Atlas Shrugged*, was a great admirer of Mickey's work and of Mickey himself. They were close friends and carried on a long correspondence. Rand once wrote, "Spillane gives me the feeling of hearing a military band in a public park."

Mickey still writes on a regular schedule. He has an office in his house and another on the deck outside the library.

After his divorce from Mary Ann Pearce, Mickey had a brief second marriage to Sherri Malinou. Malinou, an actress, had been the model on the cover of some of Mickey's books. She worked around the world through most of the marriage while Mickey remained in South Carolina.

In 1982, Sherri and Mickey divorced and Mickey met his present wife, Jane. They've been married for nineteen years.

I asked, "Did you always want to be a writer?"

"I wanted to be a pilot when I was about twelve, maybe younger," he said.

He lived within biking distance of Newark Airport in Elizabeth, New Jersey. The airport was just a big empty field with three buildings on it. He ran errands for the pilots, stole parts for their planes and brought them baskets of apples and pears. After about a year, the fourteen-year-old told one of the pilots that he wanted to fly. The pilot had an old World War I plane. He gave the boy six hours of dual flight, then let him fly solo.

When the war came, Mickey became a flight instructor working up and down both the Atlantic and Pacific coasts.

A little known fact about Mickey, the man with the archetypal tough guy image, is that he has been a Jehovah's Witness since he was baptized in 1951. He still goes door-to-door with the Watchtower and attends meetings regularly. Two on Sunday—ten and noon—plus bible

study on Tuesday nights, and on Thursday nights he goes to two meetings, a combined service and Bible school meeting.

Mickey, the most famous spokesperson for a beer company, doesn't drink anything stronger than a gallon of milk a day.

We sit in Mickey's yard facing the water and he tells me to fire questions at him.

Kaminsky: John Wayne gave you a Jaguar?
Spillane: Forty-eight years ago. It has 30,000 miles on it. It's in the garage. I don't drive it. I drive a Ford pickup.

Why did John Wayne give you a car?
Because I rewrote a movie he was producing and I acted in *Ring of Fire*, a circus picture.

You wrote a lot of pulp novels, like the Nick Carters back in the 1930's and 1940's. How many?
I don't remember. I wrote under different names.

Is Mike Hammer coming back? It's been twenty years since the last one.
I've got a new one, *The Shrinking Island*. Number fourteen for Hammer. He gets married in this one.

What are your politics?
I don't have any. I don't vote. I'm a nothing. My wife is a conservative. I didn't even vote for Ronald Reagan and I knew him for more than fifty years. I used to say, "Hi Ron," when he was president, and he'd say, "Hi Mickey."

How did you meet Jane?
She was my daughter's friend. I used to kick her out of the house when she was a little girl. I remember when we got married—that was twenty years ago—the *National Inquirer* said: Mickey Spillane marries his daughter's childhood chum.

Well that was true wasn't it?
Jane and my daughter were friends, but Jane had gotten divorced from her husband in

160

Connecticut. The family had a summer house over there, across the road. I didn't know I was in a marrying mood. We got married at the Lodge here in town.

You have a birthday coming up. How are you going to celebrate?
We're not. We don't celebrate birthdays, or Christmas.

Are there things you'd like to do but can't?
I'd like to fly. I've got a commercial license and eleven thousand miles in the air, but I'm too old. And I'm sorry I never got to do extreme skiing. I still ski on chicken little hills when we're up north in the Adirondacks. We've got a house up there that's a kind of cross between a log cabin and a Swiss chalet. We've got skis and snowshoes.

Have you ever gotten into fights with other writers?
Almost got into a fight with William Manchester. He got half drunk and said some things I didn't like. I told him if he said one more word I'd belt him. And the guy who wrote *Deliverance*, James Dickey. The public television station here was in debt and wanted the biggest South

Carolina writer to open their fundraising show. They asked me and I said, "Sure." Dickey hit the roof, and I understand he hated my guts till the day he died.

Where do you shop?
For clothes? L.L. Bean and other catalogues. I have one suit. It's over ten years old.

Do you collect anything?
Toys. Cars, trucks, airplanes. I have little bitty cars and big cars. Most of them are upstairs. I don't let my grandchildren touch them.

As we finished, Mickey Spillane walked me down to look at his boat.

MICHAEL CONNELLY

But that is the beauty of art and why we study and celebrate it. Each painting is a window to the artist's soul and imagination. No matter how dark and disturbing, his vision is what sets him apart and makes his paintings unique. What happens to me with Bosch is that the paintings serve to carry me into the artist's soul and I sense the torment.
—Penelope Fitzgerald in *A Darkness More Than Night* by Michael Connelly

We are sitting in the small office on the second floor of my home in Sarasota, Florida. Coincidentally, Michael Connelly's mother lives in Sarasota, and Michael, his wife and his baby recently moved from Los Angeles back to Florida's Gulf Coast.

Through the window of my office, we can see the leaves of a single tree. There is no vista.

"I like to be near water," says Michael looking out the window. "Feel a need for it, but I like to work in tunnel-like spaces with fluorescent lights, no distractions."

If Michael has a passion, outside of writing and his family, it is fishing. It's not surprising that fishing and water are frequent motifs in his novels.

"I'm sure one of the reasons I eventually became a writer was because of my father's love for the visual arts," Michael says. "My father was a frustrated visual artist, graduated from the Philadelphia Visual Institute of Arts. He was very artistic, but he was also practical. When I

was twelve, my mother, father, my five siblings and I moved to Ft. Lauderdale where my dad became a homebuilder. I started doing illustrations for my high school newspaper. I guess I was drawn to the movies. I began to read books on movie directors even though I didn't have anything specific in mind."

Michael worked for his father and assumed he would become a homebuilder after he graduated from the University of Florida. His major was building construction.

And then something happened. Michael transferred into the School of Journalism with a minor in creative writing.

"Some people know they wanted to be writers when they were twelve or younger," he says. "I didn't know it till I was in my twenties."

Michael's mother was a mystery fan. Agatha Christie was her favorite. Michael had read the Christie series, but always considered them 'mom books.' He read *The Hardy Boys* and in high school even wrote a mystery story which he doesn't remember but which his mother still has.

"I can't say that one particular thing made me decide to become a writer," says Michael. "I remember when I was a high school freshman, I picked a Mickey Spillane novel off of the turnstile at a drugstore. I think it was *The Erector Set* and what got me was the art work, a beautiful naked woman on the cover, her body parts covered by the book title.

"I later found out that the woman on the cover was Mickey's wife. I hid the Spillane inside a Hardy Boys book and read it in the library. The librarian caught me and took the Spillane away. It opened up the idea that there are so many different kinds of books out there. It certainly contributed to my eventual decision to be a writer. But there were other books too, like Joe Wambaugh's *The New Centurions*. It was powerful."

But it wasn't just the novelists who led Michael to his interest in the mystery and writing.

"What was more influential," he says, "was television—Rockford, Kojak, Mannix—and the metro section of the newspapers. South Florida was and is crime ridden and fascinating.

"I even had a personal encounter with a shooting and a robbery when I was sixteen," he says. "I was driving home one night and saw a man running down the street with something in his hand. I had a pretty good look at him. He threw it in some bushes and kept running, ran right into a biker bar. This was in Ft. Lauderdale. I checked the bushes and found a gun wrapped in a shirt. My father came. We called the cops who took every biker in the bar into custody for a line-up. I couldn't identify the guy. He must have left while the police were on the way.

"The police thought I was afraid to identify the guy. I remember a detective named Phil Monday browbeating me. Ten years later when I was a reporter, I ran into Monday, told him who I was and that I really hadn't been able to identify the guy. By the way, they never caught the shooter."

I say, "Personal experience, reading mystery novels and the news, watching cop shows on television all contributed to your wanting to be a writer, but was there any turning point?"

"One, I guess," he says. "I went to a movie at the Student Union, *The Long Goodbye*, the Robert Altman one. I know purists hate that movie, but it was my first encounter with Raymond Chandler. I read all of Raymond Chandler in the next two weeks. When I moved to Los Angeles, I seriously considered renting the apartment in the Hightower Apartment building they used in the movie, but there was no air conditioning and parking was almost impossible."

Another movie that influenced Michael was *Dirty Harry*. "There's more than a little Dirty Harry in Harry Bosch," he says. "Things go in circles. A few years ago, Eastwood made a movie from my novel *Blood Work* and played my detective McCaleb." The character, Harry Bosch, who he refers to has become one of the most memorable characters in crime fiction. Michael's first novel, the Edgar winning *The Black Echo* featured the Hieronymous "Harry" Bosch. Harry, stubborn, complex, deeply troubled, tough and compassionate, came to life for millions of readers and moved Michael to the bestseller list where he has deservedly remained.

The *New York Times* called him "infernally ingenious" and the *Los Angeles Times* said he belonged to "the top rank of a new generation of crime writers."

Michael's strength lies in his ability to bring to life and make the reader interested in not only Harry but all the characters—from killers to drug dealers and cleaning ladies. The same holds true of his non-Harry novels.

"Who do you envision as playing Harry Bosch?" I ask.

"I don't really think that way," he says. "But I think Steve McQueen would have been right as Harry. I think he was perfect in *Bullit*."

"What about the woman in *Void Moon*?"

"That was my one book with a female protagonist," he says. "I saw a movie and adopted the look of my protagonist from an actress who had a small role, maybe five minutes, but there was something about her look and her hardness that I liked. Warner Brothers bought it. We'll see what, if anything, they do with it."

Michael's father is dead, but he had a twin brother, a priest who Michael used as a research source for his novel *The Poet*.

"Both of my parents were Catholic," he says. "But we didn't practice, though I did go through Catholic schools. I really don't have much interest in formal religion, though I do, as readers of my books know, think a lot about the philosophy of religion. I have a lot of religion in my books, a lot of soul searching. I can't say I'm a believer or not a believer. I'm a wonderer. I think that kind of wondering became more relevant in my books since I became a father."

"Your wife agree?"

"My wife is Christian and we're raising our daughter as a Christian, but my wife and I don't really talk about formal religion. We've been married for seventeen years and I don't even know what denomination she is."

"Your name is obviously Irish."

"Yes," he says. "My family roots are in County Cork, but my parents and siblings attitude toward Ireland are similar to our feeling about Catholicism. None of us has any real desire to visit the 'old country.' I'd much rather go back to Italy."

"Are you close to your family, your sisters and brothers?"

"We're scattered all over the country," he says. "I'm the second oldest. I have three sisters and two brothers: one in Boulder, Colorado, the others in Seattle, Washington, D.C., Chicago and Miami. When I go on a book tour I try to see all of them, and we have a family reunion in Sarasota every year. I haven't missed any of those."

Kaminsky: Let's move to how you work. When do you write and how much do you try to get done each day or week?
Connelly: Depends. On a good day, I don't need an alarm. I get up around 4:30 or five and stop at eleven A.M. if I have what I hoped to get when I woke up that morning.

How many pages in those six hours?
I used to try to write five or six pages a day but I've become a binge writer. I find myself spending a lot more time thinking about what I'm going to do and not doing it and then, when I do sit down to work, it happens fast.

Do you think about what you are working on after you stop for the day?
All the time. When I'm watching television, before I go to sleep, while I'm sleeping, while I'm having dinner or lunch. I have to really be involved in something, playing racquetball, fishing, playing video games with my daughter to stop from thinking about writing.

But you don't think it's a problem?
Always thinking about what I'm writing? No.

You carry a notebook?
No, but I send myself a lot of voice mails. I should carry a notebook or a small tape recorder.

Have you ever had any novels that weren't published?
My first two. I didn't get it right till the third. I was thirty-two years old.

How would you describe your sense of humor?
Hidden. I think I have a really good sense of humor. I'm not usually a laugh-out-loud person. My books are serious, hard-boiled, but there are moments of humor in my work and I do laugh out loud when I read them.

Michael Connelly

You're a best-selling author, a former Mystery Writers of America President, and Edgar Allan Poe award winner. How does your success affect you?
I'm doing much better than I deserve. There's a built-in unfairness to that. I'm pretty easy going, but it does disturb me that the more I achieve, the more difficult it is for me to deal with the unfairness in the world.

Any big fears?
I wouldn't call it a fear but I do think the success I've had might be temporary. I try to build into my life the understanding that success and creativity might just go away. As a writer, I turn nothing into something and there is always a fear that the ability will get rusty or simply go away.

You have the reputation of being a quiet, laid back guy.
It's not true. I'm very driven but people don't see it, except for my family and close friends.

Harry Bosch, whose given name is Hieronymous, is driven. In some ways he is also an enigma.
Like the tormented painter for whom I named him and who is a running metaphor in the books.

Bosch, the painter, saw hell everywhere, the torment, murder and devouring of humanity by horrible creatures. So does Bosch the detective. In fact, the metaphor comes to the surface in A Darkness More Than Light *in which the paintings of Bosch become central to the solving of a murder.*
And both the real Bosch and Bosch the detective are surrounded by mystery. Where did he come from? What makes him view the world the way he does?

Would you, if it were possible, want to have dinner with the painter?
If he was forthcoming, but he might just crush me down.

What is there about Los Angeles that draws you, like Chandler, to it?
The fascination doesn't wear thin. I think you can reach a point in most cities where you get their measure and you know the place, but there's nothing new. I lived in L.A. for fourteen years and it became a different city at least three times during those years.

That was about it, but I had one last question for Michael. "You told me you couldn't talk to me today till after eleven. Was there some problem?"

"No, but I knew it would be a bad day if I didn't get at least three pages done before we talked."

"And?"

"It's been a good day."

[Michael Connelly photographed at his home.]

EVAN HUNTER/ED McBAIN

Gloria knew that someone was in her apartment the moment she unlocked the door and entered. She was reaching for her tote bag when a man's voice said, "No, don't."

* Her fingertips were an inch away from the steel butt of a .380 caliber Browning.*

* "Really," the voice said. "I wouldn't."*

—*Hark!* by Ed McBain

At his home in Connecticut, Evan Hunter (a.k.a. Ed McBain) sits at his desk in front of his computer. The room is large, airy, connected to the main house by an enclosed bridge. He got up around nine, had juice, cereal with berries as he read the newspaper, showered, dressed, crossed the bridge and was behind his desk by ten where, on a normal work day, he writes until six at night with the goal of completing forty pages a week.

"But I don't flagellate myself if I don't make that quota," he says.

A sign taped to his desk lamp reads: "It's Jeopardy, Stupid!" to remind him that the second novel in his women in jeopardy series must always be in danger.

Evan's wife Dragica's desk is across the room where she is working at her own computer. Dragica Dimitrijevic taught drama for Lee Strasberg and then ran her own off-off-Broadway theater before she met Evan.

"She knows dramatic structure," he says, "and she knows motivation, and she sometimes drives me nuts with her questions about my manuscripts. But I value everything she has to say, and I usually make the changes she suggests, and the result is a stronger book."

"Why do you live up here in Connecticut?" I ask.

"We just got back from two days in New York," he explains. "Noisy, crowded, dirty, a parody of itself. We like it here because we're surrounded by greenery, and it's quiet and peaceful, and we can work here together in harmony. It's lovely."

Evan was born Salvatore Lombino in New York City. He was named for his father's father, an immigrant from Sicily who was run over by a streetcar on First Avenue when Evan's father was still a boy.

"I was born on a blanket on our kitchen table on 120th Street and First Avenue," he says. "My Aunt Jenny delivered me. She was a midwife. That was Italian Harlem. Most of the immigrants in the neighborhood were from and around Naples. My parents were born in the United States. Oddly, when my father's brother had a baby, he also named him Salvatore Lombino. My father was a postman, never made more than eight dollars a week, but always had enough to take me to the Apollo Theater on Saturday nights to listen to the big bands."

Evan doesn't consider himself an Italian-American. He reads a quote from the protagonist in his 1992 87th Precinct novel *Kiss*: "When we insist on calling fourth generation native-born sons and daughters of long-ago immigrants 'Italian-Americans' or 'Polish-Americans' or 'Spanish-Americans' or 'Irish-Americans' or, worst of all, 'African-Americans' then we are stealing from them their very American-ness. We are telling them that if their forebear came from another nation, they would never be true Americans here in this land of the free and home of the brave. They would forever and merely remain wops, polacks, spics, micks or niggers."

In 1952, Salvatore Lombino legally changed his name to Evan Hunter, who then split off into the highly popular author of the 87th Precinct novels, Ed McBain. Evan Hunter writes novels. Ed McBain writes mysteries. The two personas wrote one novel, *Candyland*, together and Evan has said recently that more and more often Hunter and McBain sound alike.

Evan has three children from his first wife Anita Melnick and one stepdaughter from his second wife Mary Vann Finley. He married Dragica in 1997.

Before joining the Navy in World War II, Evan was studying art at Cooper Union. While he was a sailor he began writing. After his discharge, he decided to change direction, earned his college degree with a Phi Beta Kappa at Hunter College in New York. He taught high school in the Bronx for a few months and then found a job working in a literary agency by day and writing at night and on weekends.

His first success came in 1954 with the publication of *The Blackboard Jungle*.

Over the past fifty years since that first book, his work has been published in twenty-four countries. He has received many awards including the Grand Master Award of the Mystery Writers of America, and he was the first American to win the British Crime Writers Association Cartier Diamond Dagger.

"The book that launched your career was *The Blackboard Jungle*. What did you think of the movie version?"

"True to the spirit but not the letter of the book, but a good movie in all, despite the enormous ego of the director, Richard Brooks."

"What about some of the other movies made from your books?"

"I thought *Strangers When We Meet* was a slick Hollywood production of an essentially good screenplay, my first for the big screen. *Buddwing* wasn't bad but the screenwriters hoked it up. I'd rank *Every Little Crook and Nanny* as the worst film ever made in the history of movies. And my very good screenplay of *Fuzz* was screwed up by a first-time director, Richard Colla, by allowing his actors to improvise all over the lot. He just didn't get it."

"You wrote the screenplay for *The Birds* for Alfred Hitchcock. What was it like working with him?

"Stimulating," Evan says after a short pause. "Boring. Intense. Casual. Friendly. Adversarial. Always challenging. I learned a lot."

There have been fifty-four 87th Precinct novels. The series began when the success of *The Blackboard Jungle* prompted Pocket Books to offer Evan a three-book contract for a proposed 87th series. There have been two television series based on the 87th Precinct novels and several

theatrical movies, the first of which, based on the first 87th Precinct novel *Cop Hater,* starred Robert Loggia as Steve Carella.

"The Deaf Man," I say. "The nemesis of the 87th who has gotten away with murder for almost forty years. Will he ever be caught?"

Evan shrugs.

The 87th's have been called "police procedurals." Some admirers and fans have said that they created their own genre, a genre which I, as one of the biggest, if not *the* biggest, fan of the series have embraced. My Porfiry Rostnikov series set in Russia is shamelessly based on the 87th's. Some hallmarks of the genre are the examination of multiple crimes by a team of detectives who function like a professional family, an explanation of the private lives of the members of the team and how professional and private identity affect each other.

"I think," Evan says, "Anthony Boucher writing in the *New York Times* invented the term

'police procedural.' I hate that label. It makes a novel about cops sound like something dull and plodding.

"It's my opinion that every good novel should be a mystery. The reader should constantly want to know what is going to happen next. It's called suspense. The suspense in my novels is premised on whether or not the hero or heroine will get killed. The blinding flash comes not through insight but from the muzzle of a gun."

One of the frequent raps against mysteries is that novels are supposed to be about change, perception or insight by the central character or characters.

"Alright, but suppose," Evan says leaning back, "the perception is simply the realization that the person will never change. Or suppose that the hero or heroine remains unchanged in the novel, but his or her experience results in a profound change in the reader?"

"The reviews of your novels have generally been very good," I say. "Is there anything reviewers say about your Ed McBain books you don't like?"

"Crime novels in general get a condescending rap," he says. "'Transcends the genre' are the three most obscene words in the English language."

The 87th Precinct novels are set in the fictional city of Isola, a city suspiciously like New York flipped over physically. Evan explains that when he began the series he thought it would be easier to create his own city than deal with a real one. He now thinks he may have been wrong. One of the difficulties, he says, is that he has to remember all the streets, districts, parks and statues in a city that doesn't exist. There has even been a book *The Boys of Grover Street* put out by Bowling Green Popular Press to keep all the people and places of Isola straight.

"Why did you start the Matthew Hope series?"

"God knows," he answers. "I was living in Sarasota, Florida at the time, had just finished an 87th Precinct book and decided maybe it was time for another series, one about a lawyer in Florida. The Hopes never did as well as the 87[th]s, and they were much harder to write because of all the legal stuff. And I never got as much money for them. Now readers tell me they miss him. Where were these readers when I needed them?"

"There were thirteen Matthew Hope novels," I say. "The last one was *The Last Best Hope*. Is it the last Matthew Hope novel you'll write?"

"Probably," he answers. "Hope and Steve Carella are together in that book. Incidentally, I think the very best mystery novel I ever wrote is *There Was A Little Girl*, a Matthew Hope novel with a circus background."

"You look good," I say. "How is your health?"

"Great. Had a tumor in my neck. It's almost completely gone. Eight prior tumors in my lungs are now down to only three, which are shrunken to infinitesimal size. Chemotherapy is still underway. I feel terrific. No side effects, robust, healthy."

Kaminsky: Do ideas just strike you, play around in your head and start putting themselves together or do you plot things out like a puzzle, putting story lines together before you begin?
Hunter: I usually start with a title and a vague idea. I plot about three chapters into it, and then leap in. The title keeps me focused. When I run out of steam, I plot a little more ahead. Rewrite every inch of the way. Eventually it all falls into place. If I'm lucky.

You've written novels, short stories, screenplays and plays. Which do you like best and why?
Novels. The freedom to write what I wish to write, without interference from anyone and without constrictions of time and length. The short story is next. Hardly any market nowadays, but back then it was thrilling to be able to capture a smashing idea in 1,500 to 5,000 words. It still is when the opportunity presents itself. Theater, but I never seem to get anything produced, even though I think I write some of the best dialogue in the business. And television . . . it's the pits.

What is your favorite food?
Italian, natch.

Your favorite country and city outside the United States?
Italy and Paris. Ah, Paris.

You mentioned a contract you have with your readers. What are some of the things in the contract?
The contract is simple. Among other things, I promise I'll never bore you silly with long descriptions of winding roads through remote forests. I promise I will never write tiresome interior monologues that serve no purpose but to examine my own navel. I promise you dialogue that ain't real but that sounds real. I promise you men and women who love (and sometimes lose), men and women who break the law (and sometimes win), men and women who are confronted on a daily basis with urgent problems they must solve. Just like you and me, come to think of it.

Anything else in the contract you want to add?
I promise to keep you awake all night. I promise to keep writing till the day I die.

We're done, but I remind Evan of one of the most satisfying memories of my life as a writer. I won the Edgar Allan Poe Award of the Mystery Writers of America in 1988 for Best Novel. When the award was handed to me in front of more than a thousand people, one person, Evan Hunter, rose from his table and with a huge grin hurried to the podium and with clear unconditional warmth hugged me. The book was one of my series of police novels set in Russia, a series which exists only because of Evan Hunter writing as Ed McBain.

And by the way, my police inspector Porfiry Petrovich Rostnikov, like me, always carries an 87th Precinct novel in his pocket.

SARA PARETSKY

"Mr. McGraw. I am V.I. Warshawski." I pitched my voice
to penetrate the din. *"And you may not want to see me,
but I look like an angel compared to a couple of homicide
dicks who're going to be after you pretty soon . . . Hi, Mr.
Thayer,"* I added, holding out a hand. *"I'm sorry about
your son—I'm the person who found the body."*
—Indemnity Only by Sara Paretsky

It was a rainy, cold, Chicago Saturday morning in September. Sara Paretsky's protagonist, V.I. Warshawski had been through hundreds of days like this.

I parked about half a block away from Sara's house in Hyde Park on Chicago's South Side. The University of Chicago, where I once worked as Director of Public Relations, dominates Hyde Park. The community, which is racially mixed and solidly middle class, is bordered on one side by Lake Michigan and on the other three sides by African-American inner city neighborhoods.

The three-story brownstone house hadn't changed in the eighteen years since I had first come here. The occasion had been a party to celebrate the publication of *Indemnity Only*, Sara's first novel which she had written in a class I taught at Northwestern University. Sara had dedicated the book to me and whenever she has spoken over the years she has never failed to give me credit for getting her started.

We have been friends from the moment we met.

Sara opened the door. Slender, comfortably dressed with a look of concern, she says, "You must be wet."

I showed her my folded umbrella and she stepped back to let me in. Then she took my jacket. The house looked essentially the same as when I first saw it, warm and welcoming, especially on this gray Chicago day.

"Courtney's downstairs," she says. "We can see him later. Would you like a cup of coffee?"

I told her I would. I've known Sara's husband Courtney as long as I've known Sara. He is a tall, lean man with a gray beard and sincere smile. Courtney was a physicist at the University of Chicago until his recent retirement. Courtney's support of his wife's work has been total and enthusiastic from her first chapter.

"Where should we talk?" she asks.

"Wherever you're comfortable."

"My office, upstairs," she says getting our coffee cups and leading the way up the wooden stairs to the top of the house.

Sara's office is spacious, efficiently decorated with a functional desk, press board bookcases, a relatively uncluttered working space with wooden walls and a pitched ceiling.

From her office window, which looks out on the rear of the house, you can see her garden: lush, green and colorful, even in the early Fall.

"I love this house and looking out at that lovely back garden," she says. "It's an oasis in a crowded city."

"You like to work in the garden?"

"I don't work the garden," she says with a laugh. "Someone comes in to do that. I just enjoy the view. I'm basically an indoor person, but I enjoy the outdoors as long as someone else is taking care of it. And I enjoy walking through the woods. My lack of enthusiasm for gardening may go back to when I was ten years old. We moved to the country. My mother wanted a garden but the weeds were as high as twelve feet and grew so fast that my brother and I had to get out there and weed every day."

She sits, sips some coffee and pauses while I turn on my tape recorder.

"Let's start at the beginning," I say. "Your family. You're originally from Kansas."

"I grew up in Eastern Kansas, Lawrence," she says after a pause and a glance down at her coffee. "My dad, whose parents were from Eastern Europe, taught at the University of Kansas. My grandparents met on a picket line for the garment workers union in New York.

"When we moved to Lawrence, my father was the first Jew hired for a tenure track position. We were like the town giraffes. We moved to Lawrence in 1951 and there were sort of unwritten laws about who could live where, so we ended up living out in the country on a farm. The family that had owned and worked the farm had died, and their kids didn't want to be farmers. So it was like growing up in the suburbs. Rex Stout had grown up where I lived, went to the same two-room school I went to."

"Were the people there aware of Stout?"

"No," Sara says shaking her head. "I remember being thirteen and sitting on the back porch eating fried green tomatoes and reading my first Rex Stout book, *The Black Mountain*. I didn't discover he was from Lawrence until years later and I suppose it made me feel that it was possible to be from Kansas and be a published author."

"Before you and your family moved to Kansas . . ."

"My dad was from New York. My mother was from downstate Illinois. They met in graduate school at the University of Iowa."

"You have four brothers?"

"Yes, the oldest converted to Catholicism and became a Dominican priest. He's fifty-seven. I'm the youngest at fifty-four. Another brother is a veterinarian. Another stayed in Kansas and is an astronomer. The next one is brilliant but not good at finishing things. He works as a janitor and is still finishing his Ph.D."

"How did you get to Hyde Park?"

"My parents were a combination of socially progressive and traditional values," she says. "They didn't expect much from me other than to get married and raise a family. I decided to go to the University of Chicago."

The rain is thumping gently and steadily on the roof and we take a long detour in our conversation. Sara is interested in my family background, my health, my plans. She leans forward, asks questions and listens carefully, nodding occasionally in acknowledgement.

I change the subject from me to a low nearby shelf filled with photographs, a tiny tractor, the small statue of a woman and some objects I can't identify.

She looks at the statue and says, "That shelf is a shrine to my father, who died a few years ago. I keep working on it. The statue is Our Lady of Guadeloupe. I write messages to her. The photograph there is of my father in New Guinea when he was in the Army during World War II. And that's my parents on their wedding day. Before the war, during the Depression, my father made pocket money hustling people with chess games on the boardwalk at Coney Island where his family lived. Before he died, he turned back to his religion and became close friends with a rabbi in Lawrence. When my dad died a few years ago, the rabbi gave me the fringes from my father's Talis, the cape that men wear during religious services. I'm making a doorway in this little box with the fringes hanging as a kind of doorway between life and who knows what comes after."

"And that little table?'

"His books and coffee."

"And this small toy tractor?"

"In the country my dad grew up in a two-room cold water flat in Coney Island. He wanted to be a farmer but he couldn't figure out how to work any of the equipment when we moved to Kansas. He liked driving around on it but when any work had to be done, his students, who were farm boys, came out and did it."

I point to an object on the shelf. "And what's that?"

"It's a silver angel with wings that flop. I wish there were some way I could hook her up so her wings keep flapping without having to wind her up."

I look up at her. Her eyes fixed on the angel, her thoughts for the moment somewhere else.

"I hate people dying," she says almost to herself. And then to me, "Courtney always says, 'Sara, just think how cluttered the world would be with creepy old people if they didn't die.'"

"You write about people dying."

"I think one of the appeals of the mystery novel is that you get this kind of vicarious experience of death and dying and that someone makes it safe and distant. It's not going to happen to you because you've experienced it by writing about it or reading it."

"What writers do you read and remember?"

We move downstairs for more coffee and keep talking while Sara answers, "Jane Austen, Charles Dickens and Michael Gilbert."

"Not many people know about Gilbert," I say as we move down the narrow wooden stairway.

"He's a great mystery writer. I met him and told him how much I liked his work. I don't think he believed me till I started talking about each book and what I liked in it."

"When you appear in public or in interviews, you appear serious, confident. Is that the way you see yourself?"

Sara lets out a very small laugh, fingers her coffee cup and says, choosing her words carefully, "I think the public perception of me is someone who is very forceful. The fact is that I'm not very self-confident. I have a very hard time knowing what I want and then speaking up for it. I think things over before I speak and I keep trying to turn off the 'good girl' so I can say what I want to say. I need a balance in my life between being caring and firmly responsive. I have a high need to please others. It's not a desire. It's a need, an obsession."

"So, you're not as confident as you present yourself?"

"Right," she says changing positions in her chair, her left hand held up as she considers her answer. "When I go on stage in public—"

"You are a terrific speaker."

"I know that. People tell me and I can feel it, but I don't know where it comes from or how I make it happen."

"You prepare when you speak."

"Yes, very hard. I can be good off the top of my head but I prefer to be prepared. I taught a course in the writing program at Northwestern University a few years ago and I really prepared for those classes."

"Did you have nightmares the night before each class?"

"No, but a friend of Courtney's who retired when he was sixty, said he would always wake up during the night before a lecture with attacks of anxiety. I do dream. My anxiety dreams are that I'm being chased or, one that is really odd, I'm riding in a car cut in half sitting with other people on a narrow bench, afraid we'll all fall into the street."

"I like that one." I continue, "You travel a lot in the United States and Europe. Do you have a favorite city or town?"

"I basically like to stay at home, but I'd say my favorite city is Edinburgh, Scotland. We have lots of friends there mostly through Courtney who had to travel there frequently for science conferences."

"You're very thin, but I've seen you put away a lot of food."

"I like to eat. I eat way too much sugar. I can put away five deserts in one sitting."

"Ethnic foods?"

"I like Indian food a lot, spicy Indian food. I create my own curry. I also like Italian food. I love any kind of seafood in Italy. I don't like heavy foods. French food tends to be too heavy."

It is still raining but not as hard as earlier. Through the downpour, the sun is making a feeble effort to make its presence known.

I ask, "The last time I was here there was a big, friendly dog. Where is he?"

"She died from bone cancer," Sara says. "Courtney really needs a dog in his life, so we'll get another Golden Retriever."

"You're a Cubs fan."

"I am an insane, heartbroken Cubs fan. My most salient characteristic is probably my loyalty."

"You have a favorite team. Do you have a favorite movie?"

"Well, *Night of the Hunter*, the one with Robert Mitchum as the killer preacher and Lillian Gish as the old woman trying to protect two little children from him. I can't watch that when I'm alone in the house. I just freak out. And Beckett is one of my all-time favorites. Richard Burton's voice . . . I once got a tape of Burton reading John Donne love poems. I was driving my car when I first listened to it and almost drove off the road. I had to turn off the tape."

Sara gets up to stretch. She has a chronic back problem and likes to keep limber. She walks to the window.

The rain is letting up as we move to the front door after we find Courtney and I say hello to him.

"Have you ever written a book that you think is perfect or almost perfect?" I ask.

Sara doesn't hesitate. "No. I always wish my books were perfect and when they're not I think, 'If they were perfect, there wouldn't be anything to make me go on and try again.' So if you've written a perfect first one, you're in trouble. You just keep writing and you try not to worry about posterity. I remember once you said in class, 'Write what you want to write now. If you try to write for immortality, you'll fail.'"

JOSEPH WAMBAUGH

In the desert you don't get very much mileage from your fuel. When you're walking, that is. You can get about ten good miles out of your body if you fill your body tank with a gallon of water. You get lots less if you're wearing a navy-blue police uniform and Sam Browne, lugging a 9mm pistol and a hideout gun in a leg holster.

Especially if you have a severely sprained ankle and don't know diddly about the desert in the first place.
— The Secrets of Harry Bright *by Joseph Wambaugh*

Joe Wambaugh and his wife Dee live on a hillside high above and looking down at San Diego harbor. For about twenty minutes we watched the ships coming and departing from the well-manicured lawn behind his house.

Dee is visiting her mother in Palm Springs for the day and night. Our plan is to talk, take a tour of San Diego and have dinner with friends—cop friends—at a favorite Italian restaurant.

I haven't seen Joe in about six years. At that time, he had just finished a non-fiction book, *Fire Lover*. He would soon be named a Grand Master by the Mystery Writers of America.

"What did you do for six years?" I ask as we sit on chairs looking at the harbor.

"I played with my dogs, took them to the beach, read, tried to find a good movie on television," he says with a shrug. "I worked out on my treadmill, did some free weights. I didn't have any ideas, didn't think I had another book in me, definitely not a novel. I was shocked when this new book about an arsonist started to jell. It's non-fiction. Not only did I wind up with a book but a 600-page book. I couldn't believe it when I finally finished."

"You had a contract?"

"No, I did it on spec. It's probably going to be a problem when it comes out."

"Why?"

"I've been sued for defamation with all of my non-fiction books except one," he says. "Fighting the suits can be exhausting."

"Which one didn't you get sued for?"

"*The Blooding*," he says. "All the people in it are British. England, like every other civilized western country except the United States, has a law that if you sue and lose, you pay all the legal costs of the person you sued."

I hear a sound from the house on our right, behind some low shrubs.

"Frankie Laine lives there," says Joe. "He's ninety, still sings when he gets a few people together. It's ironic. The first record I owned, one my parents gave me because I asked for it, was "Mule Train," an old seventy-eight rpm. I played it on an old wind-up Victrola, one of those with a megaphone."

"I wonder if he watches reruns of *Rawhide*," I say. "Listens to himself singing the theme song."

"And *Blazing Saddles*," Joe adds.

Two large black dogs lope along the lawn and stand next to Joe.

"This is Zoe," he says. "She's a giant schnauzer and Joey there is a Portuguese water dog. We have a third dog, Trooper. He's a standard schnauzer. He's with Dee at her mother's."

We go back inside the house to Joe's office. The manuscript pages for *Fire Lover* are neatly stacked on the desk in his office waiting to be mailed. Bookcases and photographs line the wall. A large typewriter sits on the desk.

"You don't use a computer?"

"No," he says. "I don't even know how to turn one on. When I was working on the book, the walls and bookcases were completely covered with brown butcher paper. The doors on both sides were covered. I tape the paper all over and then do little notes and stick them on the paper or write notes directly on the butcher paper. And the floor was filled with boxes of police reports, fire department reports, reports from Alcohol, Tobacco and Firearms, somewhere between 4,000 and 5,000 pages of court transcripts. I kept it all chronologically straight on that butcher paper. The floor was covered. You could barely get through this place. No one could come in. Nobody. Definitely not the housekeeper."

"What did you use to keep the notes on the wall organized?"

"Different color pens and all those Scotch tape notes," he says. "I've done all my books that way. Pretty primitive huh?"

"It works for you," I say. "And how much do you work each day when you're on a book, this book?"

"All day, every day and usually after dinner. I want to get to the second draft, get the first one out of the way. The second draft is fun."

I agree, and we move out of the house to the driveway where we get into Joe's sports car and head down the hill toward the city.

"Let's talk about your family history," I say.

"Sure. I'm from Pittsburgh. Three of my grandparents were from Ireland, the fourth, my father's father, was from Germany. Wambaugh is a corruption of a German name, Wabach."

"Your mother's maiden name?"

"Malloy. I had two Malloy grandparents and a Connelly and a Derkin," he says as we drive. "I grew up with Irish Catholics who worked in the steel mills and factories, all blue collar. I was an only child."

"Are you a practicing Catholic?"

"I wasn't for a while, but now I'm a regular at Mass. I go to a Portuguese Catholic Church. I can't understand a word they're saying and that's the way I like it, the way I remember it as a kid when everything was in Latin. I'm getting closer to the shroud and I'd like to have a priest at my side when I go."

Joe's family moved to California in 1951 when he was thirteen. His mother's brother, Pat Malloy, was drafted during World War II even though he was thirty-eight years old at the time. He hadn't even gotten through the eighth grade, but the Army gave him an IQ test and made him an officer. When Pat got out of the Army in California, he married a woman who had some money and they bought a chicken farm.

"Uncle Pat got drunk one night, drove across a highway and got hit and killed by an eighteen-wheeler. We came out here to bury him."

"What did your father do when you moved out here?"

"He thought he would take over and run the ranch and the land, but Pat's wife turned out to be a crazy bitch. Dad had been a cop in Pittsburgh. In California, he scrounged around, got blue-collar work, repaired washing machines, stuff like that. My dad's name was Joe, too. I'm a junior. My mom's name was Ann."

Joe is a movie lover and he wants me to see the hotel where *Some Like It Hot,* a movie we both like, was shot. We park in the lot and walk to the hotel, which looks pretty much the way it does in the movie. It's bustling with people and the interior is perfectly maintained echoing the 1920's. There is a corridor of photographs taken during the making of the movie.

We are having a drink in the hotel bar when Joe begins telling me about his time in the service. "When I was seventeen, I got permission from my parents to join the Marines. I was in the Corps for three years. I was a typist stationed in Jacksonville, Florida and in California. I started taking college courses when I was in the Marines." When Joe got out of the Marines, he enrolled at Los Angeles State College under the GI Bill and worked nights in the Kaiser Steel plant as a fireman while he got his B.A. in English.

"And when you got out of the Marines, you got married. Tell me about your wife's background."

"Her family were Oakies," he says. "Dee was born in Deming, New Mexico, when her family was on the move to California. She was born in a little shack with a dirt floor. Her mother was fourteen and her father nineteen."

"Any siblings?"

"Two brothers," says Joe. "One's a murderer and one's a millionaire. The one who's a murderer killed the man who poisoned his dog. He's in prison in Central California. Dee and her mother visit him. I never have, but I do send him books and other things. He's been in so long he doesn't want to get out."

"So you don't go to prisons for research?"

"I do. I visited Lon, the main character in *Fire Lover* in federal prison. I don't make friends with crooks. I won't romanticize crooks."

We've finished our drinks and head back to the car.

"You have children?"

"Two, both adopted. My daughter lives in the L.A. area and has a daughter. My son is divorced. He does promotions for stores that claim they're going out of business. It's a bit sleazy, and my son's an alcoholic. He has a little boy. So I've got two grandchildren, and we do get to see them."

On the way back to the house, Joe says that he had planned to be a teacher. He had enrolled in an M.A. program. Until he saw an ad in the *Los Angeles Times* and realized that policemen were getting paid more than teachers.

"So I thought I'd give it a try and keep working for my M.A. I liked being a cop. It was interesting, exciting, good pension plan. I thought I could put in twenty years, get forty percent of my salary and at the age of forty-three I could be a teacher. In 1968, after thirteen years in college classes, I got my M.A."

"Did you think about writing when you became a cop?"

"I just wanted to be a detective. I was promoted to sergeant and didn't want to go any higher than that. I wanted to stay on the streets, go out on my own."

"What did you learn from those years as a cop?"

"Cynicism," he says. "That was the toughest part. You don't just deal with the worst people, you deal with ordinary people at their worst. You get to the point where you don't think anyone is worth a damn."

"The suicide rate among cops is high," I say. "You've written quite a bit about that."

"I worked with three female cops who shot themselves," he says. "Women don't usually shoot themselves, but female cops do it because they feel they have to be macho right to the end. A cop can get to the point where he or she thinks that people are garbage. Cynicism can be a fatal disease if it's not treated. Marriages suffer, guys start drinking, using drugs. And some of them shoot themselves, their wives, their girlfriends. It happens before they get their twenty years in. Cops can't quit easily. They have an investment in that pension.

"One of my classmates from the academy lives right up there." Joe points to the hills nearby. "He's a quadriplegic. His wife shot him and herself. She died. That was just a few years ago."

"Working on juvenile cases probably builds the cynicism fast."

"What people do to their kids is beyond belief," Wambaugh adds.

We're back at the house. It's late afternoon. I ask him how he got started writing.

"I had every intention of putting in my twenty years. I just started messing around with short stories. I wanted to get a few published, thought it would help me get a job as an English teacher later."

He wrote five but couldn't find a publisher.

"I tried everything, every schlock magazine I could think of and then, just for the hell of it, I sent a story to *The Atlantic Monthly*. They said they were going to publish it but then backed out, but a young girl at the magazine encouraged me to write a novel."

He did in three months. The novel, *The New Centurions*, was based on his experiences as a cop. *Atlantic Monthly Press* took it and published it in conjunction with *Little Brown*. Joe had no agent. One was recommended to him, but he didn't see that the agent was doing anything for him and dropped the agent. He has represented himself ever since.

"My characters are usually based on real people, composites," he explains. "My research consisted of my own experiences and later the experiences of other cops. Before I do a book, I take four cops out to dinner every week for a month and just listen to them. That's my research."

"When you were a cop, did you ever have to shoot someone?"

"No, but during the Watts riot I did fire a couple of shots to scare people off. I've had partners who did have to shoot someone."

"You left the L.A.P.D. when you began selling your books."

"I didn't plan to, but when that first novel came out in 1971 and became a Book of the Month selection, I became a police department freak. Cops didn't write books then. The chief didn't want the books published and threatened to fire me. I thought with titles like *The New Centurions* and *The Blue Knight*, the department might be happy. It didn't happen. The press got behind me and said it was a First Amendment issue. I called the third book, *The Choir Boys*. That didn't help. I left the force and haven't been on good terms with them since."

I tell him a little about my own work. "My books about two Chicago cops, Lieberman and Hanrahan wouldn't exist if it weren't for you. I wanted to write about cops as people with problems, families and a tough job to do."

"I've read your Liebermans, good books. I like the one with the stray dog who witnesses a murder."

"But you did something new, original," I say. "You didn't do police procedurals."

"No, police procedurals describes how the cop works on the job. I think I turned it around and described how the job works on the cop."

"The other thing I got from your books was that in the middle of something horrible, funny things can happen. Tragedy and comedy can co-exist. The alcoholic cop in *The Black Marble* is very funny. I remember laughing and feeling sorry for him at the same time when he kept using safety pins to hold his pockets together. I also loved the cop, Manny Lopez, in *Lines and Shadows* who keeps confusing people at odd times by saying '*Sabes que?*' It's funny. A little like Eddie Egan in *The French Connection* saying, 'Did you ever pick your toes in Poughkeepsie?'"

"Thanks," says Joe. "One of the cops in that story, Tony Quinta, is having dinner with us tonight. He was one of the older guys on that border task force."

"Did anyone influence you as a writer?"

"Definitely Truman Capote's *In Cold Blood* when I wrote *The Onion Fields*. That was the third book I wrote when I was a cop. I met Capote when we were on *The Johnny Carson Show*. He invited Dee and me to his home in Palm Springs. We went there for lunch and I told him what I was planning to write. He kept giving us screwdrivers, strong ones. Dee got dizzy and went into the bathroom to just lay on the tile floor. Truman suggested that she lie down on one of the beds. She always suspected that he just wanted to get me alone."

"That's possible."

"In any case, he gave me a great jacket blurb."

"You like any of the movies that have been made from your books?"

"Yes," he says. "The scripts I've written. *The Onion Fields* and *The Black Marble*. I wrote the script for *Fugitive Nights* as an NBC movie of the week. It was all right. I wrote a script for *The Choir Boys* and Robert Aldrich, the director, said he liked it. Then I discovered he had the script rewritten by another writer. The other writer and I both tried to get our names off the film."

"Were you happy with your television series, *Police Story*?"

"It ran five years. I left after the first three. The producers thought it was about plot, police action. I wanted it to be about character. Almost all the episodes were based on true events cops told us about."

"Let's try this," I say. "I'll give you the title of one of your books and you say the first thing that comes to mind."

"Okay."

Kaminsky: The Onion Fields.
Wambaugh: Sheer excitement, the most exciting book I have written. While I was writing it, I felt as if I was unearthing something important.

Echoes and Darkness.
Chilling. Foreboding. I remember having dinner somewhere outside of Philadelphia with one of the murderers, William Bradfield, before he was arrested for the murders of Susan Rimert and her children. The whole project was dark. Dark people involved in such a horrific crime.

The Blooding.
Discovery. I knew I was onto something very few Americans knew about—DNA and its use

in criminal investigation. I knew I was going to bring something back from England that even American cops hadn't heard of. As far as I know, it was the first book on the use of DNA as a law enforcement tool.

The New Centurions.
Labor pain, the pain of becoming reborn as something different, as a writer.

The Blue Knight.
Insurance policy. I wrote it in thirty-five days. I wanted to get a second book out quickly because I thought I was going to lose my job. *The New Centurions* hadn't come out yet. I had no idea whether it would be a success.

The Choir Boys.
The birthing process was complete. When I was finished, I knew I was a writer. I didn't have to hold back anymore because I was no longer a cop.

The Black Marble.
Indulgence. I had been to Russia. I was interested in things Russian including the Russian Orthodox Church. I simply wanted to write a cop book with a Russian background.

Harry Bright.
Personal. One of my favorites. The theme was the relationship of fathers and sons. Probably the most different from my other books. Paul Mazursky has wanted to do a film based on the book for a long time. It still might happen.

Fugitive Nights.
Palm Springs. Private eye. They came together. I wanted to write a proper mystery which I hadn't done before and haven't done since.

Finnegan's Week.
Another attempt to deal with something I knew nothing about, environmental crime. Did the interviews, got the information, wanted to do a book with a big theme, but that theme didn't amount to much. But there is an environmental crime. Dumping toxic waste in Mexico poisons a young boy. But it was a petty crime, not a grand scale one. Every time I think I'm going to write something big, it shrinks. It always gets down to something personal, a story about one or two characters.

Fire Lover.
Psychopathic personality or sociopathic. Repeated theme in my books, fiction and non-fiction. I'm fascinated by the disorder. It fascinated me from my first weeks as a cop and I return to it constantly. I've come to the conclusion that searching for the key to the psychopathic or sociopathic mind is probably hopeless. The key, if there is one, is probably going to be discovered by molecular biologists or geneticists, not by psychiatrists and psychologists who seem to have no luck in changing these people.

It's getting late and we have a dinner appointment. At the restaurant where Joe is greeted warmly by the waiters and owner, we sit down, as Joe frequently does, with a small group of friends—mostly cops. There is lots of laughing, lots of talking about police work and writing.

LAWRENCE BLOCK

"For God's sake, why kill me? I'm not your father. I'm your therapist. It makes no sense for you to kill me. You've got nothing to gain and everything to lose. It's completely irrational. It's worse than that, it's neurotically self-destructive."

"I guess I'm not cured yet."

—*Hit Man* by Lawrence Block

Lawrence Block, head shaven, mustache full, has a whimsical look on his face. He usually does. I've known Larry for more than twenty years and most of the time he wears a slight smile that suggests he is thinking of something slightly humorous and very far away.

Once when we were in Mexico at a writers' gathering, Larry chose to give a public talk dressed like a caricature of a tourist—knee-length tan shorts, a yellow Hawaiian short-sleeve shirt decorated with bright wild birds and oversized garish flowers, and a camera around his neck. The audience was filled with suited dignitaries of the region and conservatively dressed fellow writers. Larry gave a deadpan speech about the craft of writing and his love of Mexico. The audience didn't know what to make of it. Clearly they hadn't read the novels of this author whose work has ranged from hilarious comedy to horror to pornography.

Larry has a wondrous imagination and as a restless soul he is, indeed, often literally many thousands of miles away. He really does climb distant mountains, walk across deserts and go to exotic island nations with a sense of wonder. By his own account, he has been to 128 countries.

The first time I tried to get in touch with Larry because I was a fan, I was informed by a bookstore owner in New York that Larry had just gotten on a bus headed out of town.

"To where?" I asked.

"I don't know," said the proprietor. "I'm not sure he does either."

The wanderlust continues in his books with his love of touring. He can, and does, get in his car and visit thirty or more bookstores in several dozen states. He is the only writer I know who actually enjoys touring.

At the moment, however, he is in his office, a small apartment two flights up from the apartment where Larry and his wife Lynne live. The office, which he describes as "an unholy mess" looks out at the Manhattan skyline.

"I guess I've always had a wanderlust," he says glancing at the window. "Though like everything else it seems to get worse with time. There's a poem by Edna St. Vincent Millay in which she talks about trains and says there's never a train she would not want to be on no matter where it's going. Amen to that, I say, of trains and ships. I'd say it of airplanes, too, if air travel didn't get significantly more unpleasant every damned year."

"But touring? No one I know, no one, comes close to touring as much as you do and loving it, too? Why?"

"Beats me," he says shaking his head. "I enjoy touring, but I'm less and less convinced of the efficacy of book tours. I expect I'll be touring less rather than more in years to come."

"What is your favorite place in the world?"

"Well, probably the west of Ireland. I felt at home there the first time I went, and that hasn't changed. That's how I always answer this question but I'm not sure how valid it is. For one thing, my absolute favorite place is New York. That's why I live here. After that, my favorite place is anyplace I haven't been yet. Lynne and I enjoy almost every place we go, including the ones that aren't really very enjoyable."

Larry's paternal grandfather came to the United States from Budapest at the age of two. All of his other grandparents were born in the United States. His great-grandparents came from various parts of Europe—Lithuania, Germany, Alsace, Poland, the Ukraine.

"The borders kept shifting," he explains. "Still do, come to think of it."

His parents met at Cornell University. His father was an attorney who practiced law intermittently in Buffalo, New York where Larry was born in 1938 and grew up. His mother was a pianist and painter who never worked till her husband's death. Larry had a younger sister who died in 1978.

After high school in Buffalo, New York, he went to Antioch College. He knew he wanted to be a writer and while at Antioch wrote and submitted juvenilia.

"After two years at Antioch," he says. "I got a summer job at a New York literary agency, Scott Meredith, and started selling magazine fiction. By the end of the summer I decided the job was too good to give up. I dropped out of college. After a year, probably out of a reluctance to be drafted, I went back to Antioch, but by then I was writing paperback novels and couldn't take academic life seriously, if I ever had. At the end of that year, the Student Personnel Committee suggested that I might be happier elsewhere, and they were right about that."

To date, Larry has written more than fifty novels and over a hundred short stories. He has won three Edgar Allan Poe Awards, four Shamus Awards, the Diamond Dagger Award of the British Crime Writers Association and the Grandmaster Award of the Mystery Writers of America.

He began by writing short stories for pulp magazines including *Guilty*, *Trapped* and *Manhunt*.

"What was the first 'adult' book you read?"

"'Adult' is a curious modifier. I'm not sure if you mean grown-up or dirty. In either definition, I'm not sure what was first. I started reading realistic American fiction during my second or third year in high school—Wolfe, Steinbeck, Farrell, Hemingway, et al—and decided right about then that I wanted to go and do likewise."

"Big leap forward. You have children?"

"I have three daughters, and they do as they please. One's a parent liaison at a high school in Queens. One's a corporate real estate lawyer in Manhattan, and one's a manager at Capital One in Virginia. I have three granddaughters as well. All girls all the time, that's my policy."

"Where did you meet your wife Lynne?"

With a perfectly flat look, he answers, "I met her in a leather dyke bar on the waterfront. I had the feeling she'd clean up nice, and I was right."

"Let's get serious," I say. "What are your thoughts on religion? Do you believe or practice a particular religion?"

"I think," he says after a slight pause, "religion is a marvelous in the way it is designed to separate man from his higher power, and the true test of a religion's legitimacy is that it has thoroughly betrayed the principles of its founder. The best living metaphor turned up for me in Burma, where at one pagoda the holiest objects were three Buddha images, each about a foot high, which had been presented to the pagoda when it opened. As a sign of reverence and devotion, the religious would purchase sheets of gold leaf and diligently apply them to the little statues. This went on for years, so that by the time we saw the buddhas, they were shapeless blobs of gold."

"How about some quick Q and A's?"

Kaminsky: Who is your favorite writer?
Block: John O'Hara, hands down.

Who would you choose to play Larry Block in a movie?
Whoopi Goldberg. That woman can do anything.

Let's do the same for your principal characters.
This would be dream casting with no regard to box office or other considerations. Scudder: John Spencer; Tanner: Kevin Spacey; Bernie: Jerry Seinfeld; Keller: John Malkovich.

Do you like any of the movies made from your work?
I didn't like any of them, but neither did anyone else. Viewers tended to have a good time laughing throughout the movie, and then told each other it wasn't much good. Exactly. *Eight*

Million Ways to Die had fine performances by Jeff Bridges and Andy Garcia, but they were making up the script as they went along and it's confused and confusing. I've never met anyone who'd read the book first and liked the movie. *Nightmare Honeymoon* was based on my book *Deadly Honeymoon*. I can't imagine why anyone would voluntarily watch it all the way through.

Keller, your Hit Man, *collects stamps. Do you?*
Yes. Keller and I collect similarly—worldwide. We both use the same Scott catalog, and it serves us both as a checklist by circling the numbers of stamps we have. Keller takes the book along with him on his travels, in case he drops in on a stamp dealer, and so do I.

Did you ever write a play?
Just once and nothing happened to it. A woman in L.A. wanted to adapt a short story of mine so that she could direct it—and, I seem to recall, star in it. I looked at it and said okay, but I'd do the adaptation, which was no real work at all since the story was essentially a two-character one-act play in story form.

What is your favorite food in the world?
I was a vegetarian for over twenty years, but I got over it. My favorite food is rib-eye steak, black and blue.

Small Town and some of your early novels contain "pornography." How, if at all, do you define "pornography?"
Small Town has a lot of erotic content, and evidently gave some readers apoplexy and others a hard-on. How do I define pornography? Well, the classic definition of an alcoholic is someone who drinks as we do and we don't like him. You could probably work up something similar for pornography.

What's a perfect or near perfect day for Lawrence Block?
Any day above ground is close enough to perfect to make me happy.

How do you cope with the problem of aging your characters? You've been writing novels for forty-five years. Times change. Scudder changes. It seems to me Bernie doesn't.
The Scudder books are in real time. Scudder is thirty years older than when I started writing about him. Bernie's the same indeterminate age he was thirty years ago.

You've written two books on writing and given many writing seminars and workshops. Is there one piece of advice you want to pass on to would-be writers?
If you want to write fiction, the best thing you can do is take two aspirins, lie down in a dark room, and wait for the feeling to pass. If it persists, you probably ought to write a novel.

JOHN JAKES

When you stand five feet one and they have you cold, you can fight but it doesn't do a great deal of good. They bounced me between them, knocking all the sense out of me, repeating their question about Lorenzo Hunter's honeymoon hideaway. I knew, all right. But I'd be damned if I'd tell them.
—*Johnny Havoc* by John Jakes

John and his wife Rachel live on Hilton Head Island in South Carolina, where John has acted in *Barefoot in the Park*, *George Washington Slept Here* and played the challenging Jack Lemmon role in *Tribute*. As we sit in his living room, we can see a wide inland waterway flowing by and green, dense shrubbery on the other side through a large window.

Why, in a collection of pieces about best-selling mystery writers, did I decide to include the most popular and successful writer of American historical fiction of all time?

Before John became an historical novelist, he was a respected writer of science fiction and mysteries. He has published over 200 short stories, mostly mysteries.

"The first novel I sold," says John, "was a mystery, a not very good imitation of John D. MacDonald called *Gonzaga's Woman*. You can still find it floating around the Internet and you can even buy used copies, though I wouldn't buy one if I were you.

"I did a half dozen mystery novels when I started, even did one with a Nero Wolfe-like character assisted by an Archie Goodwin-like helper. I don't remember much about it, and it didn't do well. The publisher gave it the title *The Defiled Sister*. There was no defiled sister in the book."

"When you were in high school, what did you read?"

"Mysteries. I got a job shelving books in a branch of the Chicago Public Library on Broadway because I wanted to read Ellery Queen novels. At the time, you needed an adult card to read mysteries, either that or you had to work in the library. I worked in the library."

"What was the first writing you did?"

"When I was about seven, I couldn't get enough Superman comic books, so I wrote my own. A little later I started writing very strange science fiction verse. There was a column called "Line 'O Type" on the editorial page of the *Chicago Tribune*. The columnist didn't know who I was, but he ran my verses. Of course I didn't get paid."

"What was the first story you wrote?"

"I remember the first mystery story I ever wrote," he says with a smile. "I was under the spell of John Dixon Carr and his character Dr. Gideon Fell. My story took place in Illinois where I was living. The solution to the crime depended on the brilliant detective's observation of an unusually placed punctuation mark. It was terrible. I threw it away."

"What was your first sale?"

"When I was eighteen, Anthony Boucher bought a science fiction story of mine for *Fantasy and Science Fiction* magazine."

"You did have a successful series of mystery novels in the 1960's, four pretty funny books featuring a five-foot-one private detective named Johnny Havoc."

John nods. "Yes, they were paperback originals published by the now defunct Belmont Books. I always thought Mickey Rooney would have been a perfect Johnny Havoc."

John also wrote three Lou Largo mystery novels. They were published under the name William Ard, creator of the Largo series. Interestingly, Larry Block also wrote one of the Largo novels under Ard's name.

"I might still be writing mysteries if the historical novels hadn't come along," says John.

We move into the dining room for coffee and another view of the intercoastal waterway. Settled in again, I tell John that there are a series of conflicting legends about how he switched after writing fifty western, mystery, science fiction and several historical novels and 200 short stories to become best-selling historical novelist starting with the Kent family chronicles.

"I was working in Dayton, Ohio," John says sitting back, two hands around his coffee cup. "I had not yet made a living writing fiction though I had been reasonably successful as a corporate writer. I was working for an ad agency at the time. Before that I had worked at an ad agency in Rochester, New York. One of my friends in Rochester was a writer named Don Moffet. A packager, Lyle Engel was putting together a package for Pyramid Books, a series of historicals, the American Bicentennial Series. Lyle had asked Don if he wanted to write the books. Don was tied up writing a series of spy novels and suggested Lyle contact me. I had written about a half dozen historical paperbacks in the 1960's. So I was the number two choice. Lyle asked and I said I'd give it a shot."

"So, what does that do to the rights to your eight novels in the series?"

"The rights reverted to me. They're all mine."

I've known John longer than any other writer interviewed for this book. His daughter Ellen was my teaching assistant when I was a professor at Northwestern University.

John had attended Northwestern for a while when he and his parents lived on Chicago's North Side. Knowing he wanted to be a writer, he transferred to DePauw University in Indiana where he met his wife.

"She was my lab instructor in a biology class," he said. "I married the teacher and still failed the course."

"I should remind readers that one of your recent historical novels, *On Secret Service*, is a Civil

War spy thriller. I think it's my favorite of your historicals. I think it may have been overlooked as an Edgar Allan Poe nominee because you are considered a historical writer. Do you ever think of doing other kinds of writing, other creative work?"

"My love for the theater is lifelong," he says. "I started by wanting to be an actor. I've done a fair amount of stage acting and directing all my life. My second career choice, had it worked out, would have been to direct for the theater. If I had to choose to be someone else, I would probably choose Harold Prince." John has never completely abandoned his love of the theater and acting. He created a stage adaptation of *A Christmas Carol* in the 1980's which has been performed widely by university and regional theaters. He completed a new text and scenario for the Rossini-Respighi ballet *La Boutique Fantasque* which premiered in 2003.

"In any case, I've written for the stage, including an opera about Edgar Allan Poe that never got off the ground. More recently I wrote a musical version of *Great Expectations*. We produced it here on Hilton Head and showcased it in New York for a national conference of producing theaters. It will take a bigger theater since it has a cast of twenty-three."

"Why Dickens?"

"At a writers workshop a few years ago," says John, "an editor named Patrick O'Connor said, 'Popular writing is about the story. Literary writing is about the words.' Dickens told stories people loved and was a master of language. That's true about Shakespeare, too. He was a bang-up storyteller who happened to be a poetic genius. Dickens, Shakespeare, true genius."

"Have there been any other creative people in your family? Writers, musicians, artists?"

"My mother's father was born in Germany. Partly to keep from going into the army for a five-year tour, he moved to Paris to study painting. He decided he had no ability and came to America where he met my grandmother. They moved to Terre Haute, Indiana where he opened a butcher shop. He bought the hotel in town. That's where he died. The photograph of me at the back of *Homeland* shows me at a dictionary with a photograph of my grandfather, Karl Retz, on the wall behind me.

"It was hard for him," John says with a slight shake of his head. "He lived through anti-German sentiment through two wars. All of his relatives had remained in Germany. One member of the family was even a Nazi party member who worked for a while in the United States. As of today, all of my living relatives live in Germany."

"What about your father's side of the family?" I ask. "The Jakes?"

"A whole different story," he says. "The Jakes' line dates back to colonial days. One of my ancestors fought at the battle of Yorktown and was awarded land for his service."

"What's the ethnic origin of Jakes?"

"English probably, but it could have been Anglicized. There are a lot of Jacques, Huguenots, around Baltimore. My father's side of the family eventually settled in Ohio and Indiana. Three of my great-uncles fought in the Civil War. The most interesting one was Staff Sergeant Isaac Newton Jakes. He was in Sherman's army on the march through Georgia and South Carolina. As a South Carolina resident, I don't mention that too often. In any case, my father's father was a farmer."

"And your father?"

"My father started working as a wagon driver for the old Railway Express Agency at the age of sixteen. They bounced him around the country, but I was born in Chicago, Wesley Memorial

Hospital. We lived all over. When I was in the seventh grade, we moved from Toledo back to Chicago. My father was a traditional company man, started at the bottom and was running the company when he retired."

John and Rachel have four children and eleven grandchildren.

"I don't even try to keep up with birthdays," says John. "Rachel keeps it all on a computer."

"Let's talk about your writing habits."

Kaminsky: Do you have a certain number of words or pages you feel you have to get done when you sit down to write?
Jakes: When I sit down to write, I want to get a particular section done. It's not a matter of how many words or pages, but of getting that section done that I planned for that day.

What's a John Jakes work day like?
Get to the computer about eight in the morning, often in my bathrobe, take a shower around ten, then write till two in the afternoon. I used to work till four or 4:30, but I don't have the energy to do that anymore.

Health?
I had a little heart problem in 1994. It wasn't too serious but it was enough to get my attention so I've been trying to take better care of myself, exercise, rest. I go to bed a lot earlier than I used to. I'm usually on my back in bed with a book open by nine at night and then I read till ten or 10:30.

How long does it take you to write a book?
With research? Two or two and a half years. About half of that time is research, planning, outlining.

And your books tend to be long.
The manuscript of *Homeland*, before it was edited, was 2,300 pages.

How do you do your research?
For the historicals, if I'm starting a book on a new period, I read two or three secondary sources to get an overview. Then I start pouring over bibliographies to find books or articles that narrow down the search. Then I begin to think about the characters and events in the given historical period that will interest readers. For example, when I did research on the oil boom in California in the 1890's, I was fascinated by the fact that oil wells were springing up in people's backyards.

You narrow down a vast amount of information?
That's right. It's like an upside-down pyramid, very broad at the top and moves down till I'm focused on that tip on the bottom, the specific historical elements that are going to be part of the book.

Any snares in working this way?
I've always had this bad habit of putting in too much because it interests me. A good editor will read it and say, "Wait a minute, you have two paragraphs here where the story stops dead while you chat about something."

You do less of that now?
Yes, I consciously avoid those indulgences. I was working on a chapter this morning before you arrived. I reread two sentences I had written and said to myself, "Wait a minute. This is just research material plugged in. It has nothing to do with moving the story ahead." I deleted the sentences.

Writer's block?
I once asked Robert Silverberg, the great and prolific science fiction writer, if he ever had writer's block. He said, "Yes, it was on a Tuesday morning for twenty minutes." Scott Meredith, the writer and literary agent, once wrote something that has stayed with me for more than two decades. He said, 'Talent isn't a pan of water. It doesn't evaporate. I tell would-be writers that what they have is not writer's block. You don't want to write. Writing takes sacrifice, time and energy. Plow right ahead. If you'd rather go out and play golf, do it without feeling guilty but don't blame writer's block.' Even when I have the flu, I go in and write.

In the afternoon, John, Rachel, my wife and daughter and I head out for dinner.

"I kept you from getting your section written today," I say as we get up and stand near the window.

"I'll take care of it tomorrow," he says. "I know what it will be and I'm looking forward to seeing it on the page. That's what it's about, seeing it on the page."